From Frankie & Janice.
Christmas 2008.

Wonders

OF THE
World

A PHOTOGRAPHIC JOURNEY TO THE MOST CAPTIVATING SIGHTS

Published by
Kandour Limited
Monticello House
45 Russell Square
London WC1B 4JP
United Kingdom

First published 2007

10 9 8 7 6 5 4 3 2 1

Managing Editor: Ruth Urbom

Project Editor: Christina Czapiewska

Editorial Assistant: Emma Agyemang

Creative Director: Alexander Rose

Jacket Design: Alex Ingr

Design Layout: Daniel Oliver

Art Editor: David Fraser

Production Manager: Carol Titchener

Sales & Editorial Manager: Karen Lomax

Author: Karin Gutman

Additional Material: Kaspa Hazlewood

Text Copyright © Kandour Limited 2007

Design Copyright © Kandour Limited 2007

Printed and bound in Singapore

ISBN 13: 978-1-905741-49-6

A catalogue record of this book is available from the British Library

WONDERS
OF THE
WORLD

A PHOTOGRAPHIC JOURNEY TO THE MOST CAPTIVATING SIGHTS

KARIN GUTMAN

Kandour Ltd

The Colorado River flows through Yellowstone National Park

Contents

Ayers Rock	6-11
Easter Island	12-17
Grand Canyon	18-27
Great Barrier Reef	28-35
Lake Baikal	36-49
Land of the Pharaohs	50-67
Machu Picchu	68-81
Matterhorn	82-89
Meteor Craters	90-95
Niagara Falls	96-109
Northern Lights	110-121
Stonehenge	122-127
Yellowstone National Park	138-155
Useful Information	156-157
Index	158-159

AYERS ROCK, ALSO KNOWN AS ULURU

Ayers Rock

It remains for individual discovery so long as the human mind retains its capacity for wonder.

~ Rex Ingamells, Poet

THE DESERT FLORA MUST ADAPT TO THE HARSH
CONDITIONS AND RELY ON IRREGULAR RAINFALL

Nothing prepares the visitor for the sight of this massive monolith. *Uluru*, also known as *Ayers Rock*, stands 1,142 feet tall (348 m) and measures 5 miles (8 km) in diameter. Rising up from the Australian outback, the hypnotic rock formation shimmers in its shifting colors—from yellow to orange to burnt red—depending on the time of day. It is the "arkosic" sandstone, rich with crystalline minerals, that reflects the light and causes it to glow.

Ayers Rock is located in Australia's Northern Territory, in the Uluru-Kata Tjuta National Park, just 217 miles (350 km) southwest of Alice Springs. Once named after the Premier of South Australia, Sir Henry Ayers, it has since regained its indigenous name, *Uluru*. Extending 1.5 miles (2.5 km) into the ground, the rock's sedimentary bed was most likely laid down 500-600 million years ago on such a dramatic tilt that today it rests at an 85° angle. This remarkable landform is set against a relatively flat, sand-plain environment, dotted with small shrubs and large desert oaks. The caves around the base of the rock contain hundreds of paintings and carvings depicting traditional Aboriginal life and culture.

In 1872, the explorer Ernest Giles called it "*the remarkable pebble*," yet the indigenous Anangu tribes find deeper meaning and spirituality in this natural wonder. According to Aboriginal beliefs, Uluru is inhabited by ancestral beings who emerged when the world was unformed and featureless. The ancestors then created all the living species and desert features that exist today, and left their mark in designated sites around Uluru wherever they were active. The local Anangu people are believed to be their direct descendents, and they consider themselves responsible for the protection and management of the lands today.

The foundation of Anangu culture lies in *Tjukurpa*, or "creation law." There is no single English word to describe Tjukurpa's complex meaning, which covers religious, legal, and moral beliefs. It is the religious heritage of the Aborigines, explaining their origins and guiding them in their daily lives. It provides advice on important issues, including the rules on behavior and on living in harmony with each other and the natural environment. Only the traditional leaders can impart the knowledge of Tjukurpa. The rules and beliefs are not written— instead they are passed on orally through stories, songs, dances, and special ceremonies.

THE TRAIL AROUND THE BASE OF ULURU
IS 6 MILES (9.5 KM) LONG

In the words of Anangu traditional owner Barbara Tjikatu: "We learnt from our grandmothers and grandfathers and their generation. We learnt well and we have not forgotten. We've learnt from the old people of this place, and we'll always keep the Tjukurpa in our hearts and minds. We know this place—we are ninti, knowledgeable."

The Anangu people go to great efforts to teach visitors about their sacred land and the stories contained within it. Approximately 350,000 people visit the national park each year, and many undertake the steep hike up to the top, in spite of the Anangu's pleas to prohibit it. The climb crosses an important "dreaming track," causing distress to those who honor its spiritual significance. Photography is also discouraged.

"That's a really important sacred thing that you are climbing," Kunmanara, a traditional owner of Uluru, explains to potential visitors. "You shouldn't climb. It's not the proper thing."

In 1985, the then-Prime Minister of Australia, Bob Hawke, returned the title to the land to the Anangu, on condition that tourists would be permitted to climb the rounded, red rock. The Anangu then leased the land back to the government for 99 years for it to be jointly managed. The transfer of rights occurred because of the Anangu demonstrations in 1972, demanding their traditional ownership rights. By 1994, Uluru had been recognized as both a World Heritage property and a World Heritage site.

Thanks to the great respect and cooperation between the traditional Anangu owners and the Australian Federal Government, this ancient, cultural wonder continues to be maintained and enjoyed by all.

ULURU'S STUNNING COLORS INCLUDE REDS, ORANGES, YELLOWS, AND GRAYS

The impressive row of moai on Ahu Tongariki

Easter Island

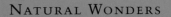

THE WORKMANSHIP IS NOT
INFERIOR TO THE BEST PLAIN PIECE
OF MASONRY WE HAVE IN ENGLAND.
THEY USE NO SORT OF CEMENT;
YET THE JOINTS ARE EXCEEDINGLY
CLOSE, AND THE STONES MORTICED
AND TENANTED ONE INTO ANOTHER,
IN A VERY ARTFUL MANNER.

~ CAPTAIN JAMES COOK,
EXPLORER, 1774

It is a small island steeped in great mystery. Covering an area of 64 square miles (165 sq km) and located 2,000 miles (3,219 km) off the coast of Chile, Easter Island, also known as *Rapa Nui or Isla de Pascua*, is one of the most isolated inhabited islands in the world. Its famous "*moai*" statues continue to raise many unanswered questions: *What is the significance behind their creation? And how were these massive stone heads transported and raised?*

Scientific studies indicate that the Polynesians first settled in Easter Island in the year 1200 AD. Almost immediately, during a period of intense creativity, they set about building these monolithic structures. Marked by angular faces and long torsos, these statues were carved out of the soft volcanic earth. Known as "*tuff*," and found in the massive caldera of Ranu Raraku, it provided a perfect material for carving. The stonework is strikingly similar to the Incan workmanship found in Machu Picchu. Examples of extraordinary and complex craftsmanship, the heads measure on average 14 feet high (4 m) and weigh 14 tons

(12.5 metric tons). The largest structure, *El Gigante* (*The Giant*), which still stands in the quarry, is 71 feet (21.5 m) tall and weighs 145-165 tons (131-150 metric tons).

Most archeologists believe that the statues represent the spirits of ancestors or the Rapa Nui chiefs, and that they may have facilitated communication with the gods. Traditional Rapa Nui folklore maintains that the "*mana*," or spiritual power, enabled the statues to "walk" from the quarry to their ceremonial resting sites. The most widely accepted theory today is that the statues were placed on wooden logrollers and moved with the help of a significant workforce. In a series of experiments, American geologist Charles Love discovered that it was possible to move a 10-ton (9 metric ton) moai 145 feet (44 m) in just a few minutes with the help of ropes and 25 men.

"The people who built these structures were both sailors and farmers, and they used their seafaring technology to help them in moving and erecting their moai," explains moai expert Jo Anne Van Tilburg of UCLA. "Erecting a

AHU VAI URI, PART OF THE TAHAI CEREMONIAL COMPLEX AT HANGA ROA

mast on a ship or a statue on a platform requires similar abilities, skills, and tools." In 1998, a documentary for PBS Nova recorded Dr. Van Tillburg's attempt to make and move an imitation moai.

Over the years, Dr. Van Tilburg has inventoried 887 monolithic statues, although there were probably more, which have disappeared as a result of erosion and other ecological changes. Ultimately, only 288 statues, or 32 percent of the total, were successfully transported to their final positions. In some cases, this would have involved a trek of 14 miles (22.4 km).

Over several centuries, the natives thrived on a lush terrain, covered with 16 million giant palm trees. The population reached 7,000 to 9,000 by 1550 AD. Yet extreme deforestation of the island ultimately took its toll. The Polynesians destroyed the trees to build their canoes, fires and most likely to move the statues. They depleted nearly all the island's natural resources, wiping out a habitat for most of the birds and animals, without concern for replenishment. While the exact details of what happened are unclear, the ensuing devastation was extensive, resulting in an eerie, barren land. By the time Dutch Captain Jacob Roggeveen arrived in 1722, the moai statues were the only remnants of Rapa Nui culture. Docking his boat on Easter Sunday, Roggeveen gave the island its current name.

"The price they paid for the way they chose to articulate their spiritual and political ideas was an island world which came to be, in many ways, but a shadow of its former natural self," said Van Tilburg.

Easter Island and its maoi statues have since become symbols of a enigmatic society that once flourished and then vanished. A cautionary tale, urging humanity to respect and live in harmony with its natural environment.

AHU TONGARIKI WAS RESTORED IN 1992
FOLLOWING THE 1960 CHILEAN EARTHQUAKE

THE RANU RARAKU QUARRY LOOKS LIKE A GRAVEYARD OF STONE GIANTS,
CONSISTING OF HALF-CARVED AND BROKEN MOAI

Grand Canyon

THE GLORIES AND THE BEAUTIES
OF FORM, COLOR AND SOUND
UNITE IN THE GRAND CANYON—
FORMS UNRIVALED EVEN BY THE
MOUNTAINS, COLORS THAT VIE WITH
THE SUNSETS, AND SOUNDS THAT
SPAN THE DIAPASON FROM TEMPEST
TO TINKLING RAINDROP, FROM
CATARACT TO BUBBLING FOUNTAIN.

~ JOHN WESLEY POWELL,
GEOLOGIST, 1869

Silence and stillness fill the air, the scenic vistas extending over one hundred miles on a clear day. It is the Grandest of Canyons—one of the world's most arresting landscapes and sublime spectacles. A step to the edge of the cliffs—and a look at one-mile vertical drop to the Colorado River below—will leave visitors reeling. Celebrated as one of the most iconic of wonders, the Grand Canyon still has the ability to surprise and amaze those who witness its splendor.

Established in 1919, Grand Canyon National Park covers 1,920 square miles (4,927 sq km). Located within the park, the Grand Canyon is a gorge of the Colorado River, extending over 277 miles (433 km) and to average depths of 4,000 feet (1,219 m). At its widest, the canyon is 15 miles (24 km) wide and its deepest point reaches 6,000 feet (1,829 m). Reaching an elevation of 8,000 feet (2,438 m) at the North Rim, the Grand Canyon is part of the Colorado Plateau, which covers parts of Colorado, New Mexico, Arizona, and Utah, extending northward into the *Grand Staircase-Escalante*. This national monument is a series of multi-colored sandstone cliffs, stretching, in order of decreasing age, from the Grand Canyon to Bryce Canyon in southern Utah. The main ridge of Bryce Canyon forms part of the distinctive "Pink Cliffs," a group of pink-or red-colored rock cliffs that have eroded into spires and pinnacles, collectively known as "Hoodoos."

Approximately 15 million people visit the Grand Canyon each year, taking in this mesmerizing force of nature. While not the biggest canyon in the world, the Grand Canyon is renowned for its well-preserved, ancient rocks, which provide an extraordinary cross-section of geological history. Forty identified rock layers line the canyon's walls, the oldest of which—the gneiss and schist found on the canyon's floor—dates back 1.8 billion years. This horizontal section of geological time covers four eras: Precambrian, Paleozoic, Mesozoic, and Cenozoic. The canyon itself is 10,000 years old. Formed by a combination of tectonic plate movement and erosion by river water, the canyon boasts five of the seven "life zones," or climates. This creates a fantastic biological diversity—the equivalent of traveling from Mexico to Canada! The semi-arid desert climate has fostered a nearly pristine environment that scientists continue to study today.

Visitors can enjoy the panoramic views from either the North or South Rims. Located 80 miles (97 km) northwest of Flagstaff, Arizona, the South Rim is easily accessible and offers stunning views from Hermits Rest, Desert View, as well as the well-known Yavapi Point in the Grand Canyon Village. Since the North Rim sits 1,000 feet (305 m) higher, it is much more difficult to reach. The Navajo Bridge is the only roadway crossing over the canyon and the Colorado River for 600 miles (965 km). Originally built in 1929 to

BRYCE CANYON WITH ITS CHARACTERISTIC SANDSTONE HOODOOS

THE SUN SETTING OVER THE GRAND CANYON

View of the Grand Canyon's South Rim

View from Yaki Point, Arizona

replace Lee's Ferry, the bridge connected the two sides at the narrowest point over Marble Canyon, a distance of 600 feet (180 m). Over time, the structure proved to be too narrow and weak for traffic, and so, a new steel arch bridge was constructed in 1995 at a cost of $15 million. The original Navajo Bridge is still open for pedestrian use and is now designated a Historic Civil Engineering Landmark.

In 1869, John Wesley Powell led the first known expedition through the Grand Canyon, via the Colorado River. Yet the region's oldest human artifacts date back 12,000 years to the Paleo-Indians. Following them, the Anasazi farmed the canyon between 700 and 1200 AD, until a severe drought drove them elsewhere. Other tribes followed, including the Hopi, Zuni, Southern Paiute, Hualapai, Havasupai, and Navajo. The native history is everywhere, most notably in the markings left behind by the different tribes. The Hopi referred to the canyon as *ongtupka*, or "ancestral home," while the Southern Paiute named it *puaxant tuyip*, or "holy land."

"All this canyon land is covered with our footprints," says Leigh Kuwanwisiwma, a Hopi representative. "It's where we had our genesis; where some of our clans farmed and lived until we were called to the mesas. It is where we make our sacred salt trek. It is where our spirits go when we die. It is where we learned the Hopi way of life, and the lessons that guide us. And the key lesson is the lesson of humility."

For 10,000 years the natives called this spiritual place home, until the establishment of the Grand Canyon National Park forced people out. The eviction of the Havasupai left them with only 518 acres (210 hectares) of land in area called Havasu Canyon. Eventually, in 1975, Congress returned 187,500 acres (75,878 hectares) of land to the tribe.

The 1,500-member Hualapai tribe recently built the Skywalk, a giant $30 million steel-and-glass walkway that opened in March 2007. It hovers over the canyon, holding only 120 people at a time. While other tribes make a living from casinos, the Hulapai live in a more remote location in the west, on a 100-million acre (404,684 hectares) stretch of land. The Skywalk juts out into the open air, putting nothing but a sheet of glass between the visitor and the abyss below. "It should be scary, but it should be really a feeling of floating out there," said architect Mark Johnson. "It's going to keep your attention." Built into

the 350 million-year-old limestone wall, which is highly prone to erosion, the structure has an uncertain future.

Beyond the scenic views, many tourists choose to venture deep into the canyon. A round-trip trek to the bottom is a 7-mile (11.3 km), one-day hike on foot, whereas rim-to-rim hikers generally take three days, stopping overnight at Phantom Ranch. The most common trails are Bright Angel and the Kaibab Trails leading 21 miles (34 km) across the canyon. Experienced backpackers will require a permit for overnight camping, but day hikers do not. Others enjoy the canyon's famous Inner Gorge rapids, where the river can drop 37 feet (11 m) in just a few hundred yards.

In addition to its buttes, spires, and mesas, the Grand Canyon hosts a variety of species, including 1,500 plant, 355 bird, 89 mammal, 47 reptile, 9 amphibian and 17 fish species. The California condor, considered one of the world's most endangered birds, is also found in this region. With a wingspan stretching 9.5 feet (3 m), this member of the vulture family has benefited from the breeding program launched by the U.S. Fish & Wildlife Service.

The natural evolution of ecosystems includes the extinction of some species and the appearance of new ones, and yet, human impact has undermined some of these natural processes in the canyon. While the overhead aircraft noise disrupts the natural quiet, air pollution from nearby metropolitan areas has brought a haze, reducing the air quality and visibility. At the same time, non-native species began to thrive in the river after the diversion tunnels around Glen Canyon Dam were closed in 1963, leading to a dramatic change in the composition of the water. As a result, the native fish were no longer spawning, and the tamarisk, an exotic shrub originally introduced to control erosion, took hold more aggressively and displaced native vegetation and animals.

Fortunately, the park's management actively addresses any threats to this revered land in order to maintain its integrity. Solutions have included no-flight zones, the eradication of harmful non-native species, and recommendations for dam modifications. Meanwhile, due to ongoing erosion, the canyon continues to expand. Yet, as the river cuts deeper into the canyon, so the Grand Canyon forever remains unaltered in our minds, ungraspable in its vastness.

VISIBILITY AVERAGES 106 MILES AND CAN
EXCEED 160 MILES ON THE CLEAREST DAYS

A DIVER EXPLORES THE GREAT BARRIER REEF

Great Barrier Reef

...EQUALLING IN BEAUTY AND
EXCELLING IN GRANDEUR THE MOST
FAVOURABLE PARTERRE OF THE
CURIOUS FLORIST...

~ MATTHEW FLINDERS, TERRA
AUSTRALIS, OCTOBER 9, 1802

You can see it from outer space—the world's largest living organism. This ecosystem is one of the most biologically diverse, home to 1,500 species of fish, 359 types of hard coral, one-third of the world's soft corals, 175 bird species, and 30 species of marine mammals. Stretching more than 1,250 miles (2,012 km) along the northeastern coast of Australia, it covers 135,000 square miles (350,000 sq km), an expanse greater than Britain and Ireland combined.

The Great Barrier Reef is made up of 3,000 coral reefs, as well as 940 islands and keys—the largest coral formation on the planet. The corals are animals, actually carnivores, related to anemones and jellyfish. While they use their tentacles to catch prey, 90 percent of their nutrients come from the golden brown algae, known as *zooxanthellae*, that live in their polyps. The corals are made up of polyps, which divide and multiply creating coral colonies. They come in a variety of forms, the most common being branching (or staghorn coral) and plate-like (table coral) colonies. Every year, on one night, over one-third of the coral population reproduces in a mass-spawning event, which usually takes place between October and December.

"Coral reefs are arguably the most complex ecosystem on the planet," says biologist Brian Huse, the executive director of Coral Reef Alliance in San Francisco. "They occupy less than one percent of the ocean, yet they are home to fully 25 percent of all marine species. And we don't even know what all is there yet: we're still identifying new species."

The first coral reefs date back as far as 500 million years ago. However, by comparison, the Great Barrier Reef is quite young—a mere 500,000 years old! Even more remarkably, according to the CRC Reef Research Center, the current reef structure is only 8,000 years old.

In 1770, the great navigator James Cook first discovered the Great Barrier Reef when his flat-bottom wooden ship, *The Endeavor*, ran into it. Cook reported in his journal, "…the Ship Struck and stuck fast. Immediately upon this we took in all our Sails, hoisted out the Boats and Sounded round the Ship and found that we had got upon the South-East Edge of a reef of Coral Rocks…"

And so the trend continued, with a reported 1,200 further shipwrecks by 1900—one of the most famous being the *HMS Pandora* in 1791, in which 30 people died. Today there are 30 shipwreck sites of historical importance located off the shores of Queensland.

Cook eventually discovered a way through this natural barrier, now referred to as Cook's passage. On August 12, 1770, Cook described the endless stretch of rocks he saw before him: "When I immediately went upon the highest hill on the Island where to my mortification I discovered a reef of Rocks laying about 2 or 3 Leagues without the Island, extending in a line NW and SE farther than I could see on which the Sea broke very high."

Today the threats confronting this organic wonder are numerous, including over-fishing, global warming, untreated sewage, and agricultural run-off from the nearby Queensland coastal croplands. Scientists estimate that 20 percent of the world's reefs are damaged, and that another 32 percent are subject to great risk over the next 30 years, if human pressures are not reduced.

A LION FISH

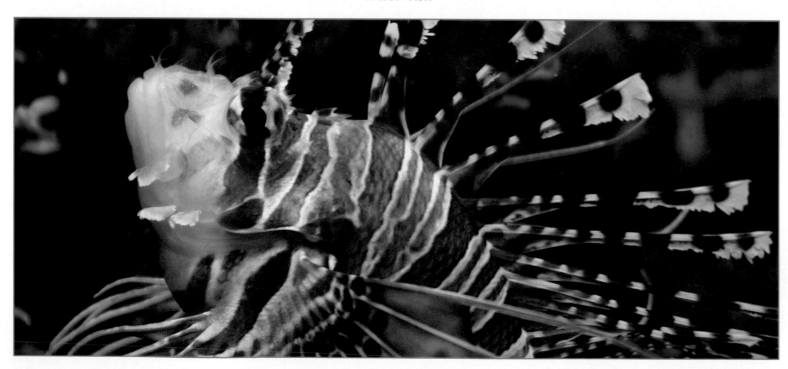

Rising temperatures, due to the effects of global warming, put the fragile coral in jeopardy. The Australian Institute of Marine Science (AIMS) reported that temperatures in Australia in 2002 were the warmest since 1870. The coral are extremely sensitive to temperature changes. This low tolerance factor causes a bleaching effect, whereby the coral lose their symbiotic algae and turn white. Prolonged bleaching can kill the coral.

"Unless the corals can adapt and become acclimatized then obviously the long-term future for the coral is at risk," says oceanographer Craig Steinberg. "The outlook isn't good. If coral can't adapt then they're going to bleach and you get mass mortality."

While algae require sunlight for the purposes of photosynthesis, too much sunlight can be toxic. It is for this reason that the coral thrives at shallow depths, where the water is warm, active, salty, and low in nutrients. That said periodic outbreaks of bleaching are normal, a part of the ebb and flow of nature's cycle. Likewise, the crown-of-thorns starfish is a natural predator of coral polyps, helping to keep the coral population in check. However, the reduction in water quality due to agricultural waste can cause the starfish to overpopulate. This disruption in the food chain can then set off a massive eradication of coral colonies. Herein lies the reality in which the fragile coral struggle to survive.

"While it's true that rising water temperatures are a big threat, you can give the coral reefs the best bet at survival by trying to remove all of these human pressures," says Helen Fox, a marine conservation scientist for the World Wildlife Fund.

In an effort to protect this marine sanctuary from exploitation, the government declared the Great Barrier Reef a Marine Park in 1975, under the new name of the Great Barrier Reef Marine Park (GBRMP). Surprisingly, more than 12 percent of land worldwide is protected, whereas less than one percent of the planet's waters enjoy the same safeguards.

"Many people thought the Great Barrier Reef was already fully protected," explains biologist Sylvia Earle, an explorer-in-residence at the National Geographic Society in Washington, D.C. "After all, terrestrial parks are not places where one expects to be allowed to cut trees, pick flowers, or kill the wildlife, and certainly not where large-scale commercial taking of the natural resources is considered normal."

Beyond its incomparable beauty, the Great Barrier Reef also supports millions of people who rely on its resources for food, coastal protection, and tourism income. At least two million tourists visit the reef each year, many enjoying the extraordinary opportunities for snorkeling, scuba diving, water sports, and bird watching. It is a destination that represents a multibillion dollar industry for Australia.

"Australia is pioneering an economy based on a healthy, thriving reef rather than one being slowly mined away," says biologist Brian Huse. "They are looking at how they can live in concert with their reefs, such that the income they generate is not damaging those reefs, ensuring that future generations will still have a Great Barrier Reef to enjoy."

THE REEF CONSISTS OF 3,000 CORALS—
THE LARGEST CORAL FORMATION ON THE PLANET

Many tourists enjoy viewing the reef from a Cessna Caravan

34

Lake Baikal

❦

Ye glorious sea, ye sacred Baikal.

~ Old Siberian song

❦

Known as the *Pearl of Siberia*, Lake Baikal is tucked away in the eastern region of Russia. It is the oldest and deepest lake in the world, containing 20 percent of the world's freshwater— more than all the Great Lakes combined. Its water basin covers 12,200 square miles (31,500 sq km) and plunges to a depth of 5,370 feet (1,637 m). By comparison, Africa's Lake Tanganyika, the world's second largest freshwater lake, is only 4,823 feet (1,470 m) deep.

This natural wonder has long been revered as one of the most sacred places in Asia, a treasure trove replete with extensive biodiversity and exceptional beauty. The lake is home to 1,500 endemic species, most notably the omul salmon and the nerpa seal, the only freshwater seal on the planet. Often referred to as "the Australia of fresh waters," largely due to its tremendous size, Lake Baikal is fed by 336 rivers and streams. Its famous crystalline waters allow for 131-164 feet (40-50 m) of clear visibility. A glimpse into its depths inspires a confidence that nature is not only alive, but thrives here. Moreover, the region surrounding the lake boasts a stunning terrain, encircled by mountain ranges and a verdant taiga, which is home to the brown bear, elk, moose, and deer. Yet, beware of the stormy winds, for Baikal is also notorious for its unpredictable, tempestuous climate.

"Woe is the wanderer who's been thrown by fate into the wave arms on a frail Baikal boat," wrote author I. Stakheyev on navigating Lake Baikal. "This boat is drifting over the sacred sea, swinging from side to side, from prow to stem, the water and ice blocks gushing into it."

Summertime, between June and August, is generally the best time to visit the region, as the winter ice usually begins in January and only thaws in May. Many come in the summer to enjoy hiking, bird watching, boating, whitewater sports, as well as the fine beaches.

While most lakes do not last beyond 25,000 or 30,000 years, Lake Baikal is estimated to be around 25-30 million years old. For this reason, scientists are drawn here to study the Baikal rift, which is a unique resource for understanding the Earth's history. Located

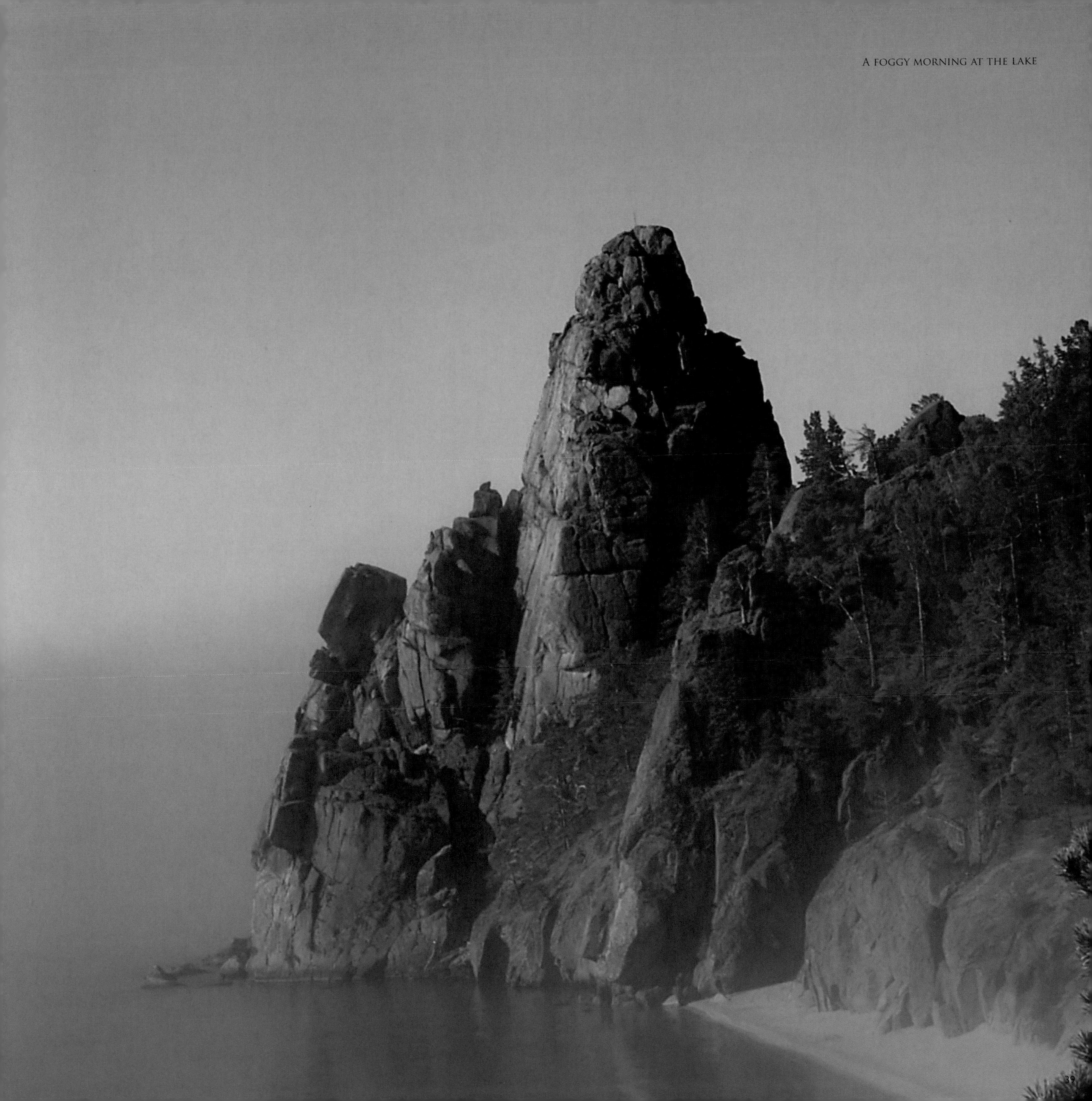
A foggy morning at the lake

on a tectonic break, Baikal's rift floor is more than five miles deep (8-9 km), making it one of the deepest active rifts in the world. Given that continental rifts are a fundamental part of the planet's geological record, Lake Baikal provides invaluable information about tectonic and climactic changes. Analyses of the ice-drilling operations that began in 1993 are expected to reveal the geological history of the region over the last five million years.

"Lake Baikal is a unique, nearly pristine environment for the study of global change," explains Dr. Steve Colman of the U.S. Geological Survey. "Nowhere else in the world can we go to study so long a record of such an important, but little known, part of the global climate system."

There is little concern that Baikal is at risk of disappearing. In fact, it is growing at a rate of 0.8 inches (2 cm) per year, causing researchers to believe that it will eventually become the next ocean.

Olkhon Island is by far Baikal's largest island. Ripe with legends and holy places, Olkhon is home to the ancient, indigenous Buryat tribes. The island's Cape Burkhan, long revered as a spiritual landmark, boasts the prominent Shaman's Rock, which is considered one of Asia's most sacred places. Olkhon legends claim that the 13th century Mongolian warrior Genghis Khan, also referred to as "Conqueror of the Universe," is buried in the cave on the western side of the cape.

"The superstitious fear that the Olkhon Buryat have towards the cave is most remarkable," explained Russian geologist Vladimir Obruchev in 1890. "It is impermissible to ride past Shamanskii Rock on wheels, but only on horseback or on a sledge; if there is a deceased person in one of the clans, a member of that clan is forbidden to ride past the cave over a particular period of time."

LEFT & RIGHT: OLD RAILROAD TUNNELS AND TRACKS OF THE CIRCUMBAIKAL RAILWAY, THE HISTORICAL PART OF THE TRANS-SIBERIAN RAILWAY

BAIKAL, THE OLDEST AND DEEPEST LAKE IN THE WORLD,
CONTAINS 20 PERCENT OF THE WORLD'S FRESH WATER

Legend has it that natives used to cover the hooves of their horses to avoid disturbing the great spirits and gods dwelling in and around this mystical place. Today, a small population of 2,000 lives on Olkhon Island in the village of Khuzhir.

Russian colonization of Siberia, a Mongolian word for *sleeping land*, took place in the 17th century. Yet Siberia remained sparsely populated—hindered by poor transportation routes—until the construction of the Trans-Siberian Railway between 1891 and 1916. Running along the southwestern coast of the lake, this network of railways connected Moscow to the Far East provinces, including Mongolia and China. Consisting of 248 bridges and 56 tunnels, the railway stretches across 5,772 miles (9,288 km) and the journey from Moscow to the East takes seven days to complete. The Circumbaikal Railway, the oldest portion of the network, took four years to build, including the construction of 200 bridges and 33 tunnels. By way of comparison, the railway is longer than both the Great Wall of China and U.S. Route 66 combined! It gave Siberian agriculture a significant boost, facilitating exports to central Russia and Europe. Today it continues to be a vital mode of transportation within Russia, carrying 30 percent of its exports.

Human activity has had an environmental impact, threatening the pristine waters, and the health of its fauna and flora. In 1999, 78 dead nerpa seals washed up on the coast, and, more recently, biologists have detected a reduced spawning rate among the omul salmon. Scientists have attributed most of the pollution problems to the construction, in 1967, of the Pulp and Paper Plant, which produces cellulose. The Russian people spoke out, ultimately motivating the Soviet government to issue a comprehensive decree in 1987 to protect Lake Baikal, forbidding shore logging and requiring the mill to undergo a review. Mikhail Grachev, a molecular biologist, then began studying Lake Baikal as the newly appointed director of the Siberian branch of the Soviet Academy of Sciences.

Despite synthetics having been proven to be more effective than cellulose, chemicals from the plant still pollute 124 square miles (321 sq km) of the lake. Moreover, the Selenga River, which provides Lake Baikal with 50 percent of its water, brings in industrial waste from Mongolian urban centers. Fortunately, despite waste dumping and noxious smoke rising, Lake Baikal is blessed with the ability to self-purify and regenerate itself, thanks to its incredible volume and depth.

Thanks to its similarity to other bodies of water, Lake Baikal has become symbolic of environmental dangers worldwide. In 1996, UNESCO added Lake Baikal to the World Heritage list, thereby strengthening its international protection and bolstering efforts to preserve this world treasure.

"Baikal is not just a lake, but something greater and deeper," says Erdeni Ulanov, Director of the Buryat National Section of UNESCO. "It is bottomless and majestic, but not an ocean or sea in which man loses all his visible bearings. There we sense the greatness of nature, feeling at one with it, not alienated from it, which is a rare phenomenon in developed countries. Baikal is a bridge to space. You must see Baikal to be able to say what it is like."

PEBBLY BEACH ON LAKE BAIKAL

PREVIOUS PAGE: SUNSET OVER OLKHON ISLAND
BELOW: IN SUMMER, VISITORS ENJOY HIKING
ON THE BEAUTIFUL CLIFFS AROUND THE LAKE

The Egyptian pyramids have become a symbol of the most enduring ancient civilization

Land of the Pharaohs

❦

THERE WAS NO TECHNOLOGY KNOWN
TO HAVE BEEN AVAILABLE TO THE
ANCIENT EGYPTIANS CAPABLE OF
ACHIEVING SUCH RESULTS. NOR
WOULD ANY STONE-CARVER TODAY
BE ABLE TO MATCH THEM, EVEN IF
HE WERE WORKING WITH THE BEST
TUNGSTEN-CARBIDE TOOLS.

~ GRAHAM HANCOCK,
FINGERPRINTS OF THE GODS, 1995

❦

THE SUN SETS OVER THE
ROOFTOPS IN CAIRO, EGYPT

Only one of the Seven Wonders of the Ancient World still exists today: *The Great Pyramid of Giza.* It has become a symbol of the most enduring civilizations in the ancient world. Ancient Egypt, also known as *The Land of the Pharaohs*, thrived along the Nile River between 3300 and 30BC. This remarkably advanced culture was renowned for its proficiency in mathematics, its well-developed irrigation techniques, and its organized bureaucracy—not to mention its invention of the calendar, based on observations of the sun and stars.

The ancient Egyptians are also credited with the earliest known form of writing. Using papyrus, a plant that grew along the Nile, they created paper-like sheets (or *papyri*) on which they wrote text called *hieroglyphics.* Meaning "sacred carving," hieroglyphics consisted of symbols and pictures that were used to represent words and concepts. They have been found on pottery dating back as early as 3200 BC, as well as in the form of Pyramid Texts inscribed in royal tombs between 2500 and 2300 BC. Scribes were tasked with keeping records and writing all correspondence, and, as a result, they left behind instructional texts for mathematics and medicine. On average, it took a scribe 12 years to learn the many hundreds of hieroglyphics of Egyptian script.

The translation of hieroglyphics remained a mystery until 1822, when French scholar Jean-François Champollion first deciphered the language on the Rosetta Stone and brought this ancient world to life. Champollion described it as "a complex system, writing figurative, symbolic and phonetic all at once." The oldest known literary work, the *Prisse Papyrus*, dating from 2000 BC, is now housed in the *Bibliothèque Nationale* (National Library) in Paris.

Papyrus documents also outlined the plans to build the Pyramids, by far the greatest imprint left behind by the ancient Egyptians. These extraordinary monuments served as the royal tombs for the kings and queens (or *Pharaohs*) of Egypt, while also functioning as places of worship. Egyptians believed the office of the Pharaoh to be divine. The monarch's burial, and the ceremonies that accompanied it, would ensure that his presence and duties continued in the afterlife. Since part of the Pharaoh's spirit, known as *ka*, was believed to stay with the body, great care was taken to prepare for this transition by mummifying the remains and placing them in elaborate burial chambers. The tombs, called *mastabas*, were initially carved into bedrock, but later evolved into the pyramidal structure. It is thought that because the triangular form reflected the rays of the sun, the deceased would be brought closer to the heavens.

THE GREAT PYRAMIDS IN EGYPT

TOURISTS OFTEN VISIT THE GIZA PLATEAU ON CAMELBACK

THE GIZA PLATEAU

More than 100 pyramids have been identified in Egypt. Most of these were built during the Old Kingdom (2575-2134 BC), which is considered to be the Golden Age of pyramid construction. Imhotep, Pharaoh Djoser's chief architect, is credited with building the first pyramid at Saqqara in 2630 BC. Known as The Step Pyramid, it began as a traditional *mastaba*, but then gained an extra six stepped layers, ultimately standing 204 feet (62 m) high. Inside, Pyramid Texts lined the walls—a collection of hymns, spells, religious instructions, and rituals. Outside, a 30-foot (10 m) wall encircled the pyramid, forming a complex that included courtyards, temples, and chapels. In total, it covered nearly 40 acres (16 hectares)—the size of a large town at the time!

Pharaoh Snefru eventually built the first "true" pyramid featuring the classic, smooth-sided lines. After two failed attempts, he ordered the construction of The Red Pyramid in Dahshur in 2600 BC. This stunning creation measured 341 feet high (104 m) and laid the foundation for the masterpieces yet to come—inspiring Snefru's son, Khufu, to seek even greater heights.

And so the Giza Plateau was born. Experts estimate that 20,000-30,000 workers built the 11 Giza pyramids over a span of 80 years. Located just outside of the modern city of Cairo, Giza became home to the largest pyramid ever built—The Great Pyramid, also known as *Cheops*. Erected in 2550 BC for Pharaoh Khufu, Cheops stands at 481 feet (147 m), and was the tallest building in the world until the Eiffel Tower was built in 1889. It took 23 years to place its 2.3 million stone blocks, each weighing on average 2.5 tons (2.2 metric tons). The granite, limestone, and basalt materials were quarried just south of Cheops. Radiating a white brilliance, a high-quality limestone graced the outer casing with some blocks weighing 25 tons (22.5 metric tons) each. Without access to modern-day machinery, it is difficult to fathom how this ancient culture accomplished such an extraordinary feat of engineering. The workers would have had to set a block every 2.5 minutes! Many originally thought that Khufu used slaves to do the work, but experts have since disproved this theory.

A PHARAOH'S HEAD

56

Egyptian bas-reliefs in the Temple of Kom Ombo

Archaeologists now maintain that the Egyptians conscripted workers, most likely during the periods when the Nile was flooded.

Any attempt by contemporary archaeologists to reconstruct a pyramid, using ancient materials and tools, has only led to more confusion and amazement. The structural precision is equally mystifying. "The Great Pyramid is extremely accurately aligned towards North," says Dr. Kate Spence, a British Egyptologist. "The sides deviate from true north by less than three arc minutes, that's less than a twentieth of a degree, which is extremely accurate in terms of orientation."

Next to The Great Pyramid, stands *Chephren*. The second pyramid to be built on the Giza Plateau, it was created in 2520 BC for Khufu's son, Pharaoh Khafre. While appearing taller than Cheops—because it is on higher ground— Chephren is actually ten feet smaller at 471 feet (144 m). The surrounding complex included the typical elements associated with pyramids, but also an unprecedented number of statues, including The Sphinx. This iconic, royal sculpture is part man, part lion. Carved directly into the limestone plateau, it measures 66 feet tall (20 m) and 164 feet long (50 m)—the largest freestanding sculpture that survives from the ancient world. Its missing nose is blamed on a stray cannonball launched during Napoleon Bonaparte's invasion of Egypt in 1798. Over the years, the statue became buried in sand up to its neck, until the first modern dig in 1817. It was not until 1925 that the entire Sphinx was finally uncovered and underwent restoration.

The last of the three great pyramids on Giza Plateau, *Menkaure*, was left unfinished, probably due to Pharaoh Menkaure's sudden death. While it was considerably smaller at 213 feet high (65 m), it contained some of the

BELOW: THE PYRAMIDS AT GIZA, BUILT DURING
THE OLD KINGDOM (2575-2134 BC)
LEFT AND RIGHT: EGYPTIAN HIEROGLYPHICS

finest sculptures. The Pyramids at Giza were typically unornamented, yet one of the most beautiful tombs is that of Meresankh III, which contains wonderful bas-reliefs. This method of sculpting, which predates sculpture in the round, carves out images from the stone, projecting the figures and scenes out of the background. The end of Menkaure's dynasty marked a downturn in pyramid building, just when Egyptian civilization reached its zenith—its population soaring to 3-4 million between 1550 and 1070 BC. Pyramid construction moved from Giza to Saqqara and diminished in quality, possibly due to the combination of financial strain and hostile neighbors. Ultimately, the ancient Egyptian kingdom would disappear, eventually becoming part of the Roman Empire.

Three millennia of significant contributions to humanity remain the legacy of Ancient Egypt. Credited with inventing philosophy and science, ancient Egypt has also provided the world with core religious and artistic values. Despite being an extinct civilization, The Land of the Pharaohs remains imprinted on the world's consciousness, embedded in our everyday.

THE CHEPHREN PYRAMID BUILT FOR PHARAOH KHAFRE IN GIZA, EGYPT
PREVIOUS PAGE: ELEMENTS OF EGYPTIAN HISTORY ILLUSTRATED ON PAPYRUS

CARVED DIRECTLY INTO THE LIMESTONE, THE SPHINX IS THE LARGEST
FREESTANDING SCULPTURE SURVIVING FROM THE ANCIENT WORLD

THE SPHINX: PART MAN, PART LION

THE STEP PYRAMID AT SAQQARA STANDS 204 FEET (62 M) TALL

A sunset and the Giza Pyramids

Machu Picchu

Something from an idyllic dream—an ancient city suspended above the clouds.

~ Johan Reinhard, Anthropologist

This sacred city seized the world's attention in 1911, when archeologist Hiram Bingham stumbled upon it. He was searching for Vilcabamba, the last undiscovered stronghold of the Incan Empire, which was destroyed by the Spanish invaders in 1572. Instead, Bingham found an extraordinary incline of ancient terraces built into the side of the mountaintop.

"Suddenly I was standing in front of the walls of a ruin and houses form the best quality of Inca building art," explained Bingham, who documented his findings in *Lost City of the Incas*. "The walls were difficult to see because the trees and moss ranked partly the stones during centuries. But in the shade of bamboo bushes and climbing plants were the walls visible of white granite blocks chopped in the highest precision. I found brilliant temples, royal houses, a big square and tens of houses. It looked like a dream."

Machu Picchu, meaning *Old Peak*, is one of the Inca's best-kept secrets—no written records document its existence. Who lived there and why it was built remains a mystery. Many believe this pre-Columbian ruin was a royal estate and religious sanctuary for the Inca ruling classes. Archeologists estimate it was built around 1450 AD, by Sapa Inca Pachacuti, and inhabited for a century, hosting a population of between 300–1,000 people at any given time. Around the time of the Spanish conquest, it fell into disuse and "disappeared." No one knows exactly what happened, but it is clear that the Spanish conquistadors never did find the citadel. Herein lies the great enigma of the Lost City.

Located 44 miles (70 km) northwest of Cuzco, Peru, Machu Picchu sits atop a ridge high in the Andes Mountains at an altitude of 8,000 feet (2,438 m). Nestled between two mountain peaks, above the Urubamba River valley, it is surrounded by an impressive gorge and subtropical rainforest. The silhouette of *Huayna Picchu*, or "Young Peak," stands prominently in the background, resembling the face of an Inca looking upwards towards the sky. From

THE AGRICULTURAL TERRACES

A FOGGY SUNRISE OVER MACHU PICCHU

here, many enjoy the astounding view of the citadel and the entire valley. In his poem *The Heights of Machu Picchu*, Pablo Neruda called it "one of the great marvels of South America."

The cloud-shrouded, misty shrines are accessed via the Inca Trail. This extensive and complex network of Incan roads covered 14,000 miles (22,500 km) converging at Cuzco, the capital of the Incan Empire. *Camino Real*, or "Royal Road," is the most important artery, stretching over 3,230 miles (5,200 km). Today, thousands of tourists walk the Incan roads, following the Inca Trail to reach Machu Picchu. There are three different route options that vary in altitude and length. Ranging from a two-day to four-day trek, all routes lead through the Andes Mountains, well-preserved Incan ruins, and sections of the Amazon rainforest. All roads eventually converge at *Intipata*, or "the Sun Gate," which is the entrance to Machu Picchu. Buses also ferry visitors to the site from the town of Aguas Calientes.

The citadel itself is divided into three distinct sections: *agricultural*, *urban*, and *religious*. The agricultural area is a series of terraces and irrigation channels, whose aesthetic purpose appears to have outweighed their practical uses, with the exception of cultivating maize and cocoa. At least 50 species of orchid also thrive in the region, watered by the numerous fountains. Representative of an extensive irrigation system, these fountains highlight the Incan aptitude for advanced urban planning.

The engineering of the landscape is remarkable. Machu Picchu's giant walls, terraces, and stairways were carved out of the mountain's gray granite—making this citadel a stupendous architectural achievement. The network of approximately 200 buildings included palaces, temples, baths, cosmic observatories, and residences. Given that the Incas did not use the wheel, it is hard to imagine how they transported the blocks of stone. Many archaeologists believe that groups of men pushed them up the mountainside. More than 100 flights of stone steps line the vertical precipice, which descends 1,968 feet (600 m) to the river valley. The cut stones fit together so tightly that no mortar was necessary—not even a knife could fit through the precise edges. Considered a wonder of both

THE SKILLED STONEWORK—GAPS FORMING
DUE TO SIGNIFICANT MOVEMENT

architectural and artistic genius, the complex stone masonry was also praised by Bingham: "What an extraordinary people the builders of Machu Picchu must have been to have constructed, without steel implements, and using only stone hammers and wedges, the wonderful city of refuge on the mountain top."

Located in the religious quarter, The Temple of the Sun is a circular tower that exhibits the best stonework. Its base forms a cavern known as The Royal Tomb, where the Incas are thought to have kept and worshipped mummies of their ancestors and the high imperial dignitaries. Above all, the mountaintop sanctuary fulfilled spiritual functions, and so the mausoleums carved in rock were the most spectacular and luxurious. Also located within the sacred district, *Intihuantana*, meaning "for tying the sun," is a stone column the size of a grand piano. Archeologists believe the Incas held ceremonies around this prominent site just before the winter solstice, in order to prevent the sun from disappearing. This natural rock formation may have been an astronomical observatory, a type of sundial tracking time and dates, or perhaps an altar to worship the Incan deities. Shamanic legends believe that access to the spirit world can be gained by touching the stone with the forehead.

In 2002, Peruvian archaeologists uncovered the first full burial site at Machu Picchu. "When the citadel of Machu Picchu was discovered in 1911, 172 tombs with human remains were found, but over the years only bones have been found," explains Fernando Astete, Machu Picchu's administrator. "It's only now that a complete burial site has been uncovered." The archaeologists also discovered funeral objects at the site, including well-preserved ceramics, a stone pan and clay pot.

The burial site has since been put on display to encourage tourism. Visitor numbers now exceed 500,000 per year. According to UNESCO, people traveling the 30-mile Inca Trail to Machu Picchu soared from 6,000 in 1984 to 66,000 in 1998. Due to concerns about over-use, the Peruvian government

MACHU PICCHU SITS BETWEEN TWO MOUNTAIN PEAKS
ABOVE THE URUBAMBA RIVER

has limited the number of hikers to 500 per day, forcing tourists to book their trips in advance. The greatest concern, however, is that a massive landslide could send the stone ruins crashing down into the Urubamba valley below. Japanese geologists have been studying the site and have documented significant movement, which is beginning to cause gaps in the stonework. Nonetheless, the cash-strapped Andean nation is still considering installing a cable car on the mountain incline to boost tourist numbers.

In 1983, Machu Picchu became a World Heritage site. The effort made to preserve these stones is ultimately an attempt to preserve the mystery and magic of pre-Hispanic life. "Above all, there is the fascination of finding here and there under swaying vines, or perched on top of a beetling crag, the rugged masonry of a bygone race," wrote Bingham. "And of trying to understand the bewildering romance of the ancient builders who, ages ago, sought refuge in a region which appears to have been expressly designed by nature as a sanctuary for the oppressed, a place where they might fearlessly and patiently give expression to their passion for walls of enduring beauty."

A LLAMA

MACHU PICCHU'S BUILDINGS INCLUDE PALACES,
TEMPLES, BATHS, AND COSMIC OBSERVATORIES

THE MATTERHORN IN ZERMATT, SWITZERLAND

Matterhorn

The Matterhorn is climbed for a variety of reasons, but first and foremost it is climbed because it is the Matterhorn.

~ Gaston Rebuffat, Alpinist

THE MATTERHORN, ALSO KNOWN AS MONT CERVIN, IS THE
MOST RECOGNIZED MOUNTAIN ON THE EUROPEAN CONTINENT

Nestled in the Alps, this statuesque rock pyramid reaches 14,687 feet (4,478 m) into the skies, towering over Zermatt, Switzerland. Also known as *Mont Cervin* (or *Le Cervin*), the Matterhorn boasts four sharp faces originally carved by glaciers. Its absolute symmetry has achieved iconic status as the most recognized mountain on the European continent.

"Without other nearby peaks to distract from its austere, crystalline form, the Matterhorn is incomparable, an icon of beauty and unattainability," report alpinists Hervé Barmasse and Luca Maspes in *Alpinist* magazine. "In the collective imagination, in Europe, it symbolizes all mountains."

Located on the Swiss-Italian border, the Matterhorn has attracted many mountaineers wishing to scale its unique and beautiful form. Judged "unclimbable" in 1792 by early alpine explorer Horace Bénédict de Saussure, the mountain remained invincible for years, defeating all those who attempted the climb. Nevertheless, de Saussure described the Matterhorn's "triangular obelisk" as the most beautiful sight in the region.

It was not until July 14, 1865, that British alpinist Edward Whymper and six fellow climbers conquered the Matterhorn. By comparison, Mont Blanc, the highest peak in the Alps, was successfully climbed 80 years earlier. Yet the trek up the Matterhorn proved both victorious and fatal. On the descent, after Whymper and his team had reached the peak, Robert Hadow, the most inexperienced climber in the group, slipped and fell. Because all the men were attached to the same rope, three other climbers also plunged to their deaths before the rope eventually broke. A horrified Queen Victoria reacted by nearly outlawing the sport of climbing altogether.

In his book *Scrambles Amongst the Alps*, Whymper relays a cautionary tale to those alpinists who would follow in his footsteps: "Climb if you will, but remember that courage and strength are naught without prudence, and that a momentary negligence may destroy the happiness of a lifetime. Do nothing in

WOODS IN ZERMATT, SWITZERLAND
AT THE BASE OF THE MATTERHORN

A Swiss sunset with the Matterhorn in silhouette

haste; look well to each step; and from the beginning think what may be the end."

Today the Hörnli Ridge has emerged as the most popular route, enticing more than 200 climbers each day. It normally takes two days to make the climb, which is primarily a rock route with occasional deep snow. As the climb is considered "moderate," it is not difficult for skilled mountaineers. The greatest dangers are rock falls and overcrowded routes. Furggen Ridge still proves to be the most rigorous of all the routes.

The surrounding region is exquisitely beautiful—with lush meadows and pristine landscapes. Zermatt, or *Zur Matte*, meaning "in the meadow," is a village situated at the base of the Matterhorn. Whymper's

conquest of the mountain made this town famous worldwide, so much so that the original rope from the illustrious 1865 expedition is on display in Zermatt's Matterhorn Museum. An ecologically progressive town, Zermatt is a car-free zone and, as a result, the air is fresh and the atmosphere welcoming, both for locals and visitors.

Set in a valley, Zermatt is surrounded by a ring of other impressive mountain peaks, including Dent Blanche, Weisshorn, Dom, Gabelhorn, Zinalrothorn and Monte Rosa—all towering over 13,000 feet (4,000 m). Yet it is the Matterhorn—stunning and majestic—that stands out the most. Its tall rocky fang is one of the very few peaks that has gained a legendary prominence.

AUTUMN TREES FRAME THE SNOWY PEAK

PANORAMIC VIEW OF METEOR CRATER,
ALSO KNOWN AS BARRINGER CRATER
—FLAGSTAFF, ARIZONA

Meteor Craters

THE IMPACT OF SOLID BODIES IS
THE MOST FUNDAMENTAL OF ALL
PROCESSES THAT HAVE TAKEN PLACE
ON THE TERRESTRIAL PLANETS...
COLLISION OF SMALLER OBJECTS
IS THE PROCESS BY WHICH THE
TERRESTRIAL PLANETS WERE BORN.

~ EUGENE M. SHOEMAKER,
GEOLOGIST

METEOR CRATER, LOCATED IN ARIZONA, WAS THE
FIRST TO BE RECOGNIZED AS AN IMPACT CRATER

If you have ever seen a "shooting" or "falling" star, you have witnessed a small meteoroid entering the Earth's atmosphere. While most of these distant objects spawned by asteroids and comets never actually reach the planet, there are extraordinary imprints carved in to the Earth's surface that prove otherwise. Indeed a number of these stellar objects *have* made impact.

The Meteor Crater, also known as the *Barringer Crater*, was the first terrestrial impact crater ever identified. It lies just east of Flagstaff, Arizona, measuring 4,000 feet (1,200 m) in diameter and 570 feet (170 m) deep. Experts believe that it appeared during the Pleistocene era and that it is around 50,000 years old.

The object that excavated this massive indentation was a nickel-iron meteorite around 54 yards (50 m) wide, cruising at speeds of 28,600-45,000 mph (12.8-20 km/second). The blast was equivalent to the explosion of 2.5 megatons of TNT, 150 times the force of the atomic bomb that destroyed Hiroshima. The debris showered 175 million tons of rock across 100 square miles (260 sq km) wiping out all living creatures in the immediate vicinity and leveling everything within an 8.5-13.5 mile (14-22 km) radius. The shock of the impact would have caused an earthquake of at least 5.5 on the Richter scale.

While the Meteor Crater did not cause permanent environmental changes, other impact craters have wreaked unimaginable devastation. It is now widely believed that the Chicxulub Crater, buried beneath the Yucatán Peninsula in Mexico, was the cause of the extinction of the dinosaurs 65 million years ago. Earlier, scientists had attributed these gigantic holes to volcanic activity. It was Daniel Moreau Barringer, a mining engineer, who first suggested that a violent impact formed the Meteor Crater. Barringer was so convinced of the validity of his theory that he formed the Standard Iron Company, bought the crater site, and began mining for evidence. Unaware that the meteorite had vaporized upon impact, Barringer drilled 1,376 feet (419 m) into the crater, spent millions of dollars (by today's calculations), and yet he found nothing to support his hypothesis. Even so, Barringer documented his "impact theory" and, along with mathematician and physicist Benjamin C. Tilghman, published it in the *Proceedings of the Academy of Natural Sciences*. In 1906, they also presented their hypothesis to the U.S. Geological Survey in Philadelphia.

Barringer's theories met with skepticism, and the controversy continued to brew within the scientific community. So it was not until 1960, when Eugene Shoemaker identified certain minerals in the crater—coesite and stishovite—that Barringer's impact theory was finally confirmed. The presence of these minerals could only be the result of a meteorite event, as their formation requires higher heat and pressure than volcanos could ever produce. Shoemaker also noted that the "shock-metamorphic" effects of the impact crater display distinct physical markers, such as "shattercones" and "shock lamellae" (crystal deformations).

So far, experts have identified 150 craters worldwide, the majority of which are located in North America, Europe, and Australia. The most recent crater discovery was in southwestern Egypt in 2004. Named *Kebira*, meaning "large" in Arabic, it is more than 25 times the size of Barringer's Crater, and roughly 50 million years old. Most craters are less than 600 million years old, and most tend to be three million years old or younger. Due to the effects of erosion and other geological processes, many craters are poorly preserved, which may cause a number of them to go unnoticed. Further research has been done on the Moon craters, which have suffered minimal erosion and can be studied indefinitely.

Many wonder if (or when) another crater will appear on our doorstep. Scientists believe that it is inevitable, yet, to temper any apprehension, they explain that the average gap between large impacts is around one million years. In 1908, the Tunguska impact ravaged the Siberian forest, and it is the most recent event to date. Although the asteroid completely disintegrated before touching the ground, it wiped out over 30 miles (50 km) of vegetation. The sound of the impact reached clear across the world—all the way to London!

The good news is that with modern-day technology, not only can scientists identify asteroids heading for a collision with Earth, but they also have plenty of ways to deflect the asteroid from its path. Altering an asteroid's "Yarkovsky Effect"—or the amount of heat it radiates—is one of a few options scientists are considering to change the course of an asteroid.

While scientists are looking outward to space, others gaze deep into the Meteor Crater. Today it is a popular tourist attraction, still owned by the Barringer family, and is open to visitors year round.

METEOR CRATER IS AN EXAMPLE OF A SIMPLE CRATER,
FORMING A SMOOTH BOWL SHAPE IN THE GROUND

NIAGARA FALLS

Niagara Falls

...It impressed me with a sense of its own grandeur, and of the impotence of man, more than anything I saw...

~ H. HUSSEY VIVIAN, NOTES OF A TOUR IN AMERICA, 1877

It cascades an impressive 600,000 gallons (2.2 million liters) of water per second. Plunging over a cliff of dolostone and shale, Niagara Falls are the second largest falls on Earth after Victoria Falls in southern Africa. The drop is equivalent to the height of a 20-story building and generates a thunderous noise, heard from miles around. Straddling the international border between Canada and the United States—between Ontario province and New York state—Niagara Falls attracts millions of tourists each year.

Its formation dates back to the last Ice Age, some 18,000 years ago, when Ontario was covered in polar ice sheets. The melting of the ice sheets, known as the Wisconsin Glacier, over 12,000 years ago, released vast quantities of water creating the Niagara River and the Great Lakes. One-fifth of all the fresh water in the world lies in the Great Lakes, with the four Upper Great Lakes (Michigan, Huron, Superior, and Erie), accounting for most of the water in the Niagara river. The river eventually pours over the falls into the *Niagara Escarpment*. From the bottom of the falls, the water travels a few miles through a number of gorges, eventually reaching Lake Ontario, the last Great Lake.

Contrary to popular belief, Niagara Falls is not just one waterfall, but three. Indeed, some five hundred years ago the Niagara River hit an obstacle, now known as Goat Island, causing it to split. This division created three separate falls: the American and Bridal Veil Falls on the American side and Horseshoe Falls on the Canadian side. The American Falls, also referred to as *Rainbow Falls*, extend 1,060 feet (323 m) across, while the Horseshoe Falls are far more powerful and awe-inspiring at 2,600 feet (792 m) wide. They also provide 90 percent of the total water flow over Niagara Falls.

Until the 17th century, the area remained completely undeveloped, marked by pure expansive wilderness. The first native inhabitants were the Ongiara Indian tribe, from which the name *Niagara* derives. It means "Thunder of Waters" or "Strait" in the Seneca Indian translation. The European explorers followed, led first by Étienne Brûlé.

SCENIC BINOCULARS

NIAGARA FALLS CASCADES AN IMPRESSIVE 600,000 GALLONS
(2.2 MILLION LITERS) OF WATER PER SECOND

He arrived in 1626 under the leadership of Samuel de Champlain, the founder of "New France," the first settlement in Quebec. Many of the early explorers reported hearing the roar of the falls, before they actually saw it with their own eyes.

In 1678, Father Louis Hennepin set out on a voyage to explore the western part of New France, and it was through him that the world discovered the Falls of Niagara. "Betwixt the Lake Ontario and Erie, there is a vast and prodigious Cadence of Water which falls down after a surprising and astonishing manner, insomuch that the Universe does not afford its parallel," wrote Hennepin in his book *New Discovery of a Vast Country*.

Over the years, efforts to balance commercial development with ecological preservation of the falls have proven to be a challenge. In the late 1800s, as the Industrial Revolution took hold, Niagara Falls emerged as a natural resource for hydroelectric power. Today, the Falls generate over four gigawatts of electricity, or one-quarter of all the power used in New York state and the province of Ontario.

In 1950, the United States and Canada signed the Niagara River Water Diversion Treaty to determine how much water could be diverted for the purpose of power generation. As a result, the countries agreed to build the Hydro Control Dam to reduce the water flow by 50 percent. They also agreed that both countries would enjoy the benefits from this source, as long as there was still enough water to maintain Niagara's majestic beauty. The amount of water that is re-routed depends on the time of day and season. During peak tourist season (April to November), the water flows to its maximum during daylight hours, but in the evenings the flow is reduced to restock the hydroelectric plants. Even so, the falls are enchanting at night, with spotlights illuminating them against the nighttime backdrop. The light shows have taken place every night of the year, since their inception in late 1800s.

Siphoning away some of the water serves another important purpose: to delay the effects of erosion. In 1841, British scientist Charles Lyell concluded that Niagara's gorges were receding at the rate at 3.8 feet (1.15 m) per year. By 1927, thanks to the hydroelectric diversions that reduced the water pressure, this rate had decreased to 2.3 feet (0.7 m) per year. Today the erosion rate of Horseshoe Falls is less than one foot (30 cm) annually, while the American Falls is eroding at a rate of only 3-4 inches (7.6-10 cm) every ten years. In 1969, the US Army Corps of Engineers halted the American Falls completely for several months, in order to study the rock formations and their erosion. They also took advantage of the stoppage to perform remedial work. By installing underwater weirs, the engineers successfully redirected the most damaging currents, thereby lessening erosion even more. The only other time the falls

THE LIGHT SHOWS HAVE ILLUMINATED THE FALLS
EVERY NIGHT SINCE THE LATE 1800S

Visitors sport yellow ponchos to ward off
the misty spray at Bridal Veil Falls

stopped altogether was on Easter morning in 1848 when an ice jam on the Niagara River prevented the water from advancing. Upon hearing the silence, many thought it was the end of the world!

Unfortunately, the very geological features that make Niagara Falls an ideal place to produce power, also make it vulnerable to toxic waste disposal from the hydroelectric plants. In 1984, experts estimated that 3,000 pounds (1,360 kg) of illegal waste were dumped into the Niagara waters, with deadly consequences to animal life and the region's ecosystem. The U.S. Environmental Protection Agency has organized significant campaigns to raise awareness of this problem and to fund clean-up operations.

Niagara Falls is a popular honeymoon destination, a tradition pioneered by Napoleon's brother Jerome Bonaparte—but it also attracts daredevils. Since the 1800s, a number of adventurous people have taken the plunge over the falls, some to their deaths. Sam Patch, also known as *The Yankee Leaper*, is the first person known to have survived the stunt. And so the trend continued, including 63-year-old Annie Edson Taylor, who flung herself over the cliff in a barrel in 1901. Others have attempted to cross the falls by tightrope, following the example of Jean-François "Blondin" Gravelet, who did do successfully in 1859. All the stuntpeople have performed their daring acts on the Horseshoe Falls, since a large rock, known as the *Talus*, sits at the bottom of the American Falls.

Nevertheless, the Niagara Parks Commission, established in 1885, declared it illegal to "attempt or perform any stunt or feat", and anyone violating the ban will meet with strong penalties including a fine and/or jail time!

For the more faint-hearted, a ride on one of the *Maid of Mist* boats might be more appealing. Named after an Ongiara Indian mythical character, and available from both the US and Canadian sides, these cruises have been carrying passengers under the falls since 1846. Another alternative is to venture deep into the Niagara Gorge on *The Cave of the Winds Tour*. After taking an elevator 175 feet (53 m) down into the gorge, visitors, sporting yellow ponchos and special footwear, can experience an up-close and personal view of Bridal Veil Falls. From the famous "Hurricane Deck," only 20 feet (6 m) away from the roaring torrents, the view is impressive and visitors are often soaked by the falls' spray!

So what does the future hold for this spectacular natural wonder? It is not easy to predict, beyond the certainty that the gorge will continue to erode, albeit at a reduced pace. If the falls reach as far south as Lake Erie, the falls may cease to exist entirely. Rockfalls also continue to threaten the appearance of the falls, and they may eventually reduce them to mere cascades and rapids.

Still, for now, the Falls of Niagara stand tall and proud, emanating a majestic beauty that continues to attract and inspire people the world over.

PREVIOUS PAGE: THE AMERICAN FALLS AT NIGHT
BELOW: NIAGARA FALLS SUPPLIES 25 PERCENT OF ALL POWER USED IN NEW YORK STATE AND ONTARIO PROVINCE
NEXT PAGE: "A VAST AND PRODIGIOUS CADENCE OF WATER." ~ FATHER LOUIS HENNEPIN, 1678

Northern Lights

No other natural phenomenon is so grand, so mysterious, so terrible in its unearthly splendor as this; the veil which conceals from mortal eyes the glory of the eternal throne seems drawn aside, and the awed beholder is lifted out of the atmosphere of his daily life into the immediate presence of God.

~ George Kennar, Explorer,

Siberia 1871

A sky shimmering with incandescent lights—ribbons of green, billowing curtains of yellow, a reddish glow—undulating against the nighttime backdrop. People from the around the world travel to the Earth's magnetic poles to witness this extraordinary light show. They are wondrous, that is certain. They are a natural phenomenon to marvel at, an awe-inspiring spectacle. Many gasp the first time they experience these dazzling, dancing displays.

The scientific name of this magnificent spectacle is *Aurora Borealis*, also known as the *Northern Lights*.

"Some of them have heard about it so much, they feel it's one of the things they must see before they die," says Pete Redshaw, a guide at the Chena Hot Springs Resort near Fairbanks, Alaska. "Others want to see something so magical, something so unimaginable. I've seen some people cry when they see it."

In 1911, the polar explorer Frederick Cook described himself as "spiritually intoxicated" by the aurora: "The divine fingers of the aurora, that unseen and intangible thing of flame, who comes from her mysterious throne to smile upon a benighted world, began to touch the sky with glittering, quivering lines of glowing silver."

In fact, the word *Aurora* finds its origins in the Roman Goddess of Dawn, and the Latin word *Borealis* meaning "northerly." Similar light displays also occur in the southern hemisphere, called *Aurora Australis*, or *Southern Lights*. Galileo was the first to use the term *aurora borealis* in 1619, when he likened the northern lights to the early dawn. According to seismologist Neil T. Davis, Galileo's faulty theory that the auroras were caused by the sun's reflection on Earth's atmosphere has persisted for centuries.

Early on, the myths that emerged to explain these paintings in the sky were as diverse as the cultures from which they hail. Finnish legends stated that the lights were foxes made of fire lighting the atmosphere with their dynamic tails, while the Inuits (or Eskimos) believed them to be spirits playing soccer in the sky with a walrus skull. The Algonquin held that the lights were the embodiment of their ancestors dancing around a ceremonial fire. For many natives the polar lights, especially the red ones, foretold of disaster or inclement weather. Above all, inhabitants of the auroral zones hold them in great esteem.

Like a snowflake, each aurora is unique. The full spectrum of colors ranges from green and yellow, to pink and red. Green is the most common color, because the sun particles react to the oxygen in the atmosphere by producing a green and yellowish glow. Red hues are the rarest, only occurring during a more intense storm. This potent force can stretch the auroras from the poles clear to the Equator. Their shapes usually fall in one of five basic categories: arcs, bands, patches, veils, or rays. The term "curtain" is used to describe an aurora billowing

in dramatic folds, similar to drapery, and the term "corona" indicates a band of rays emanating from a singular point in the sky. While some auroras are static and quiet, most shift and move in the night skies—their motions often described as pulsating, flickering, or flaming. The *magnetic zenith* is the term for the point at which the auroral rays appear to converge, as they move and change shapes.

Despite many documented observations of this magical phenomenon, explorers still longed for a scientific explanation for it. "Will man ever decipher the characters which the Aurora Borealis draws in fire on the dark sky?" asked Danish explorer Sophus Tromholt in 1885. "Will his eye ever penetrate the mysteries of Creation which are hidden behind this dazzling drapery of color and light?" Tromholt organized a network of northern lights observation stations during his 15-year stay in Norway, and he wrote a book about his observations entitled *Under the Rays of Aurora Borealis*, which was published in 1883.

Not until the mid-19th century did scientists make significant headway in explaining the cause of the auroras. Yet many mysterious questions remained unanswered. Eventually, a precise connection was found between the Sun's charged particles and their interaction with Earth's magnetic field. You might imagine the poles of the Earth's core as a bar magnet, deflecting any outside matter and protecting its atmosphere. Auroras occur when the Sun emits particles into space—a phenomenon called *Coronal Mass Ejections* (CMEs)—which increase in velocity due to the energy of the solar wind. It can take two to four days for the particles and solar wind to reach the Earth's magnetosphere.

"It is almost certain that the energy to power the aurora comes from the sun," explains geophysicist Dan Swift. "From the sun there is a continuous outflow of matter in the form of electrons and nuclei of atoms, mostly hydrogen nuclei (protons). This flow, called the solar wind, streams at speeds near 400 km/sec (900,000 mph) and therefore takes several days to reach the earth, whereas light takes only eight minutes."

Once they do arrive, these fast-charged particles, or electrons, enter the Earth's magnetic field at speeds of 600 miles per second (965 km/sec). Equal to 10,000 volts, it has the effect of a shockwave or an explosive burst. The particles then accelerate along the magnetic lines, pulled toward the poles, where they release their surplus energy that ultimately produces the light known as the aurora. The process is often compared to the mechanism that illuminates a neon sign. This bundle of free-range energy creates a shift in the magnetic field, also known as a "substorm," which lasts 10-30 minutes. The amount of energy released during a typical auroral event of one to three hours is equal to an earthquake of magnitude six on the Richter scale. Yet all this activity takes place 50 to 200 miles (80 to 320 km) above the Earth.

The greatest geomagnetic storm ever recorded occurred in 1859, creating an astoundingly brilliant auroral display. By far the most intense coronal mass ejection known to date, it was described in *The New York Times* as so bright that "ordinary print could be read by the light." It was the first time that a link was made between auroral activity and electricity.

There have been reports of auroras disrupting radio signals, causing them to reach farther than usual. In one example, a cab driver in Alaska received a message from a dispatcher in New Jersey! Of deeper concern, however, are the more powerful auroras that can cause serious disruption on the ground, such as blackouts and increased corrosion in oil pipelines. In space, they have also been known to damage satellites.

Auroral scientists, working closely with solar physicists, continue to study this phenomenon in order to better understand its effects and to warn power and communication companies, and the military, of any potential risks. The

LEFT: ACTIVE NORTHERN LIGHTS
BELOW: GREEN GLOW ROLLS FROM BEHIND THE TREES

A COLORFUL AURORA BOREALIS DISPLAY AT TWILIGHT
RIGHT: A PINK AURORA
NEXT PAGE: AN INCANDESCENT BAND OF NORTHERN
LIGHTS OVER THE CITYSCAPE

University of Alaska Fairbanks is one of the best equipped for auroral research. Located 110 miles (177 km) from the Arctic Circle, Fairbanks has always attracted scientists eager to study auroras. Scientific experts shoot rockets into the skies and gather data using sophisticated instruments. They also collect information via the numerous satellites that continuously monitor the activity around the Sun and its solar wind. Poker Flat Research Range, just 30 miles (48 km) outside Fairbanks, is where many of these experiments take place.

Ned Rozell, a science writer at the Geophysical Institute at the University of Alaska Fairbanks, likens studying an aurora to hunting a moose. "You know your quarry is out there," Rozell says, "but you don't know its size, or exactly when or where it will appear. You can wait for your target to bump into you, or you can stalk."

For those eager to view this spectacle with their own eyes, there are some tips to bear in mind. Most notably the higher the latitude, the more likely the auroral events. Interior Alaska and Canada are ideal for viewing the Northern Lights, and the best time of year to see them is between the months of October and March, when the nights are longest and the sky darkest. Greenland, the Scandinavian coast, and Siberia are also good viewing places. Statistically, Alaska's auroras are around 20-30 percent brighter than any other region, and Fort Yukon is known as the aurora capital of the world.

For serious aurora hunters, the University of Alaska's Geophysical Institute offers weekly forecasts, and NASA's Space Weather Bureau monitors geomagnetic activity and the probability of solar flares. Perhaps the most up-to-date source of information comes from The Space Environment Center, which provides real-time information on the position and intensity of auroral activity, including a map reporting current activity in the northern and southern hemispheres. Fortunately, today, most auroras can be forecast a day or two ahead of time. On average, most storms last more than 24 hours, but the most intense period lasts only 10-30 minutes, between the hours of 11:00 p.m. to 1:00 a.m. For those interested in capturing the auroras on camera, a wide-angle lens and a 30-second exposure at ISO 400 offer the best results.

Yet the real magic of *Aurora Borealis* can only truly be appreciated by the naked eye.

Stonehenge

❧

Our Countrymen reckon this for one of our wonders and miracles, and much they marvel from whence such huge stones were brought. I am not curious to argue and dispute, but rather to lament with much grief, that the authors of so notable a monument are buried in oblivion.

~ William Camden, historian and antiquarian, 16th century

❧

More than 1,000 prehistoric stone circles exist in Britain and Ireland, varying in size, shape and number of stones. Located 9 miles (14.5 km) north of Salisbury in southwestern England, Stonehenge is the most sophisticated stone circle in the world. This 5,000-year-old Neolithic monument is not the largest circle, but it is the only one with lintels placed horizontally atop the upright stones, making it unique in design. It is also the only circle built with stones that are not locally sourced. How the 40-ton slabs were transported from 20 mile (32 km) away remains a mystery

Using radiocarbon dating techniques, archaeologists have divided the construction of Stonehenge into three major phases over a 1,400-year period. The first phase began in 3100 BC with the building of a circular ditch containing 56 small holes, later named *Aubrey holes* after the 17th century antiquarian John Aubrey. With a series of wooden buildings at its center, the circle was aligned with the midsummer and winter solstices. This crude calendar would have allowed farmers to chart the changing seasons, spurring speculation that Stonehenge was used for astronomical purposes. They would not have been the first to do so. It is widely believed that Zorats Karer, or *Karahunj*, in Armenia was the world's first astronomical observatory dating from 7500 BC. Located in Armenia, this stone circle consists of 203 stones, the largest of which weighs 55 tons (50 metric tons). Evidence shows that this ancient astronomical gauge was in use for nearly 4,000 years.

The second major building phase began around 2500 BC, when the existing buildings were replaced with stones known as "bluestones," which form today's inner circle. The Heel Stone, measuring 16 feet high (4.9 m) and extending another 4 feet (1.2 m) into the ground, was also erected at this time. Since the bluestones came from Preseli Hills in Wales, it is hard to imagine how these stones made it to England in an age without machinery, metal tools, or the wheel! Some believe glaciers moved them part of the way during the Pleistocene era, while Arthurian legend claims that

STONEHENGE WAS CLOSED TO THE PUBLIC FOR 15 YEARS
(1985-2000)

How these 40-ton slabs were transported remains a mystery

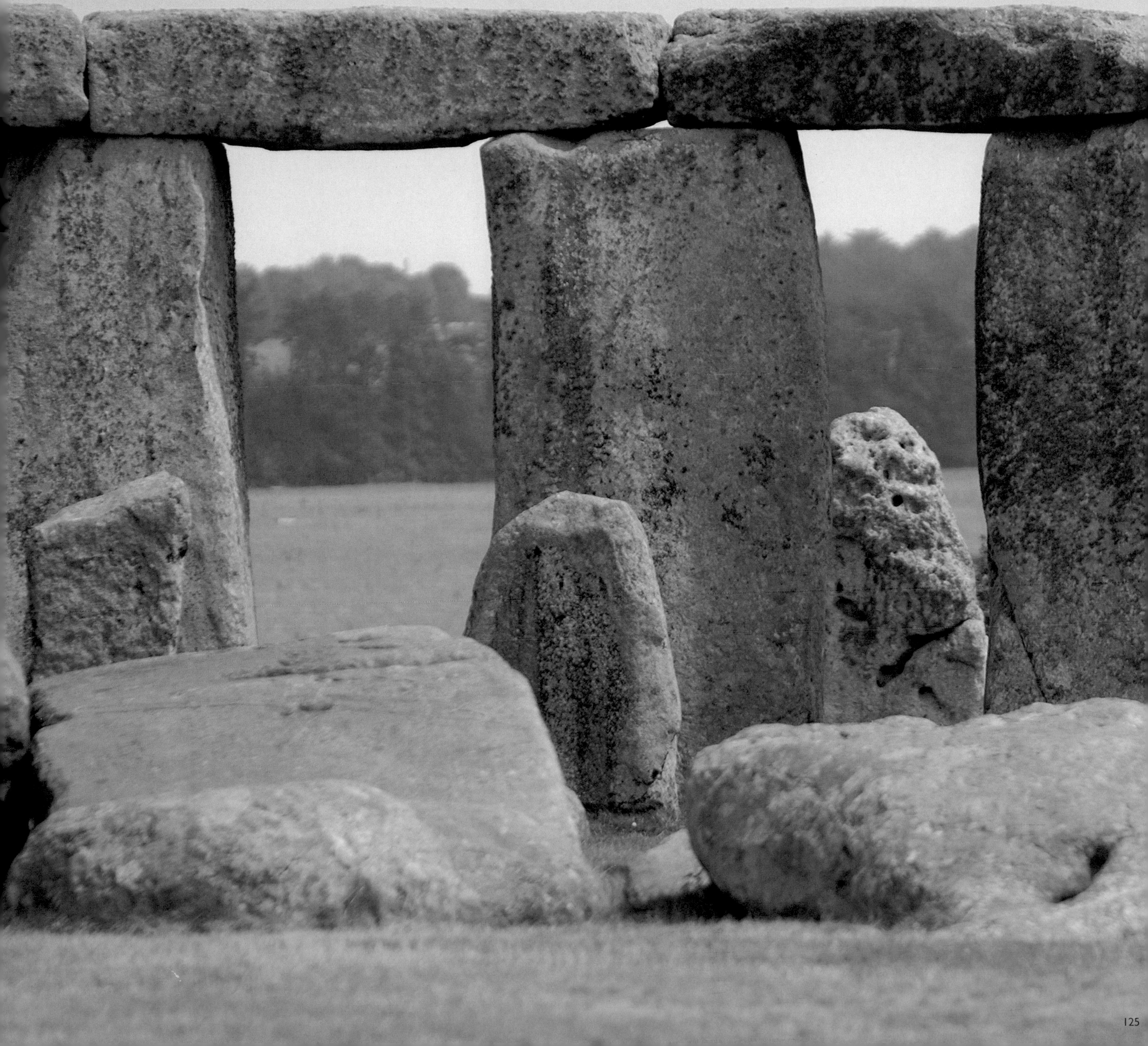

STONEHENGE WAS BUILT IN THREE MAJOR PHASES
OVER 1,400 YEARS, STARTING IN 3100 BC

after the Giants had brought them to Ireland from Africa, Merlin the Wizard moved them to Salisbury Plain.

Forming what we know as the current-day Stonehenge, the third phase spanned the years 2300-1600 BC. The bluestones were removed and replaced with sandstone rocks, known as "sarsen." The Sarsen Circle, consisting of 30 giant sarsen stones, 17 of which are still standing today, measures 108 feet (33 m) in diameter with the stones placed 3.2-4.6 feet (1-1.4 m) apart. Each stone weighs approximately 25 tons, stands 4 feet (1.2 m) tall, and measures 6.5 feet (2 m) wide. Within the Sarsen Circle stand five massive "trilithons" in the shape of a horseshoe. The trilithons consist of two upright stones with a horizontal lintel placed across the top. The tallest one measures 25 feet (7.6 m), with the average lintel measuring 10.6 feet (3.2 m) across.

Experts estimate that this last phase would have required 1.75 million man-hours over a period of 200 years, although more recent approximations suggest a shorter construction time. It is likely that the indigenous Beaker Folk of the Neolithic period built it, using antlers to dig holes into the chalky ground. Many theories still abound about how the stones were moved and raised, the most widely accepted one being the use of a sledge built from local timber. What is clear is that the large workforce responsible for this impressive engineering feat was organized and sophisticated.

The giant sarsen stones came from the Marlborough Downs, 20 miles (32 km) north, near the site of another stone circle called Avebury. Not as elaborate as Stonehenge, Avebury is however much larger. Measuring nearly one mile (1.6 km) in circumference, the outer circle has a diameter of 1,100 feet (335 m), making it one of the largest prehistoric circles in Europe. It is older than Stonehenge and four times its size. The Swindon Stone is the most impressive stone weighing in at 60 tons (54 metric tons).

Experts are not certain of the purpose behind Stonehenge. It is most likely it was used either for religious worship or as a huge astronomical calendar. In January 2007, archaeologists discovered a village, Durrington Walls, 2 miles (3.2 km) from Stonehenge, which offered deeper insight into the mystery. It is the largest Neolithic town found to date, with a diameter of 1,476 feet (450 m) and a timber circle similar to its stone equivalent at

A STORMY DAY AT STONEHENGE

Stonehenge. "Durrington is almost a mirror image of its stone counterpart at Stonehenge," says Mike Parker Pearson of the University of Sheffield. "You can pretty much overlie the plan of Stonehenge on the timber circle and see they're the same dimensions."

Built during the same period, the two sites are undoubtedly linked. While Stonehenge's avenue lines up with sunrise, Durrington's avenue lines up with the summer solstice at sunset. They also both have avenues leading to the Avon River, a fact that supports the theory of a ritualistic relationship between the two sites. Archaeologists now believe that Stonehenge was part of a much larger religious complex and that people moved between sites during ceremonies. It is likely that worshippers traveled from one to the other carrying human remains, using the river as a conduit to the underworld. "The theory is that Stonehenge is a kind of spirit home to the ancestors," Parker Pearson says.

Given that the prehistoric burial mounds surrounding Stonehenge have already been linked to mainland Europe, experts think that Stonehenge may have been an important pilgrimage destination to commemorate the dead. Durrington provides further evidence that Stonehenge had a broader function. "Rather than just focusing on Stonehenge as something in isolation," says Julian Thomas of Manchester University, "we're seeing the way in which it relates to a whole landscape."

Ritualistic celebrations are still organized at Stonehenge today. Contemporary pagans, many of whom are Druids, believe the summer solstice carries a deep mystical and religious significance, and they continue ancestral forms of celebration at what they consider a sacred place. Between 1972 and 1984, the Druids gathered at the Stonehenge Free Festival to witness the stones' alignment with the solstice sunrise. This celebration grew to attract 30,000 devotees, until a confrontation with the police caused the closure of Stonehenge. The raucous behavior of some festival goers was seen as a threat to the integrity of the monument. The 15-year ban was lifted in 2000 when English Heritage opened the grounds to 8,000 worshippers. Six

STONEHENGE IS UNIQUE BECAUSE OF ITS TRILITHONS—
TWO UPRIGHT STONES WITH A HORIZONTAL LINTEL ACROSS THE TOP

years later, this number had grown to 19,000. Open solstice celebrations have since been peaceful events. "We see Stonehenge more as a temple than as a monument," says Arthur Pendragon, a Druid leader. "Instead of wrapping it up in cotton wool, we see it as a living landscape, to be used to celebrate the seasons and quarter days [solstices and equinoxes]. Druids want to use sacred sites as they were originally intended."

Now attracting nearly one million visitors annually, Stonehenge was co-listed, with Avebury, as a World Heritage site in 1986. Yet, the large number of visitors has put a strain on the site's roads and facilities, to the point that, in 1992, the UK Parliament called it a "national disgrace." English Heritage, the charity managing the site, and The National Trust, which owns the 1,500 acres (607 hectares) of land around Stonehenge, are working with the British government to address these issues. There are plans for a new Visitor Center as well as new access roads. In the meantime, a "Stone Circle Access" system is in place to limit the number of people who can visit the site at any given time. The sole reason for these new plans and regulations is to preserve this remarkable prehistoric wonder.

Stonehenge retains the spirit of a bygone era. It symbolizes creativity, endurance, and above all mystery. "To me Stonehenge is the physical manifestation of the ingenuity, the determination, the spirituality, and the genius of our prehistoric ancestors," says archaeologist Julian Richards. "I love it, and I love the feeling that I will never fully understand it."

THE SWINDON STONE AT AVEBURY

ZORATS KARER, ALSO KNOWN AS KARAHUNJ

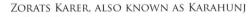

The Colorado River flows through Yellowstone National Park

Yellowstone National Park

I sat there in amazement, while my companions came up, and after that, it seemed to me it was five minutes before anyone spoke. Language is inadequate to convey a just conception of the grandeur and sublimity of this masterpiece of nature's handiwork.

~ CHARLES COOK, REFERRING TO ARTIST POINT, 1869

GRAND PRISMATIC SPRING, THE LARGEST HOT SPRING IN NORTH AMERICA

Visitors will need a few days to uncover all the gems hidden within this picturesque geological park. Yet nowhere else will they find so many natural wonders in one place!

Located in the northwest corner of Wyoming, Yellowstone National Park also extends into Montana and Idaho, straddling the Continental Divide. It covers an area of 3,468 square miles (8,983 sq km), which is equivalent to the size to the state of Connecticut. The first, and oldest, national park in the world, Yellowstone is comprised primarily of high, forested, volcanic plateaus that have been eroded over the millennia by glaciers and water. The park is famous for its thermal wonders, including geysers, hot springs, "fumaroles" (steam vents), and mudpots—not to mention its remarkable wildlife sanctuary. Home to grizzly bears, wolves, bison, and elk, the park hosts over 175 different species of birds and 600 varieties of trees and plants. Perched at 8,000 feet (2,400 m) and flanked by the Rocky Mountain ranges, Yellowstone is part of the Greater Yellowstone Ecosystem (GYE), one of largest, intact temperate zones on the planet covering an area of 18 million acres (7.3 million hectares).

The surplus of extraordinary scenery can be savored atop the Grand Canyon of Yellowstone. The great lookout spot, called "Artist Point," offers a view of Yellowstone and nature in all its grandest splendor. "There is something in the wild scenery of this valley which I cannot describe," wrote Osborne Russell, a mountaineer and author of *Journal of a Trapper*, in 1835. "But the impressions made upon my mind while gazing from a high eminence on the surrounding landscape one evening as the sun was gently gliding behind the western mountain and casting it gigantic shadows across the vale were such as time can never efface. From my own part I almost wished I could spend the remainder of my days in a place like this where happiness and contentment seemed to reign in wild romantic splendor."

Nearly three million people visit the park annually to enjoy an array of activities. The summer months attract 50 percent of tourists, who can be found mountaineering, kayaking, fishing, photographing wildlife, horseback riding, and boating. Over 1,110 miles (1,770 km) of trails provide endless paths of discovery for hikers, backpackers, and cyclists alike. Permits are required to stay overnight at one of the 300 backcountry campsites, but cannot be issued more than 48 hours in advance. In the wintertime, most park roads are closed, yet many people still come to snowmobile, snowshoe, ice-skate, and cross-country ski.

Many visitors are surprised to learn that they are standing on one of the largest active volcanoes in the world. Yellowstone's central plateau was born in a succession of volcanic eruptions, the last of which occurred some 600,000 years ago and created the "caldera," or crater top, that makes up the park. The

AN ERUPTING GEYSER

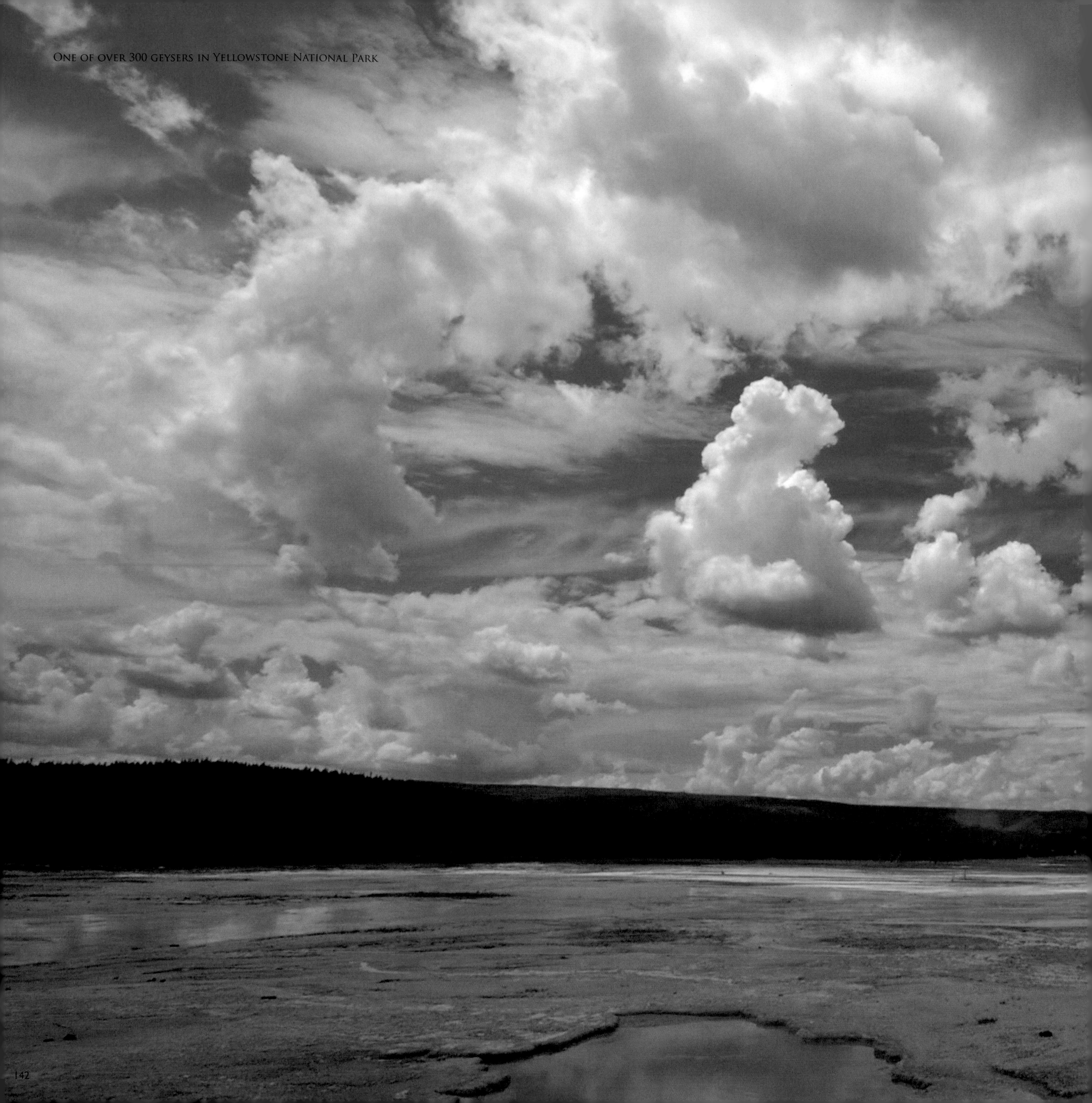

One of over 300 geysers in Yellowstone National Park

A BULL ELK BUGLING FOR HIS LADIES

A GRIZZLY BEAR

Yellowstone eruption dwarfed that of Mount St. Helens in 1980, producing 2,400 times the volume of volcanic rock. It left in its wake the Yellowstone Caldera, a crater 30 by 40 miles (50 by 60 km) wide known as the *supervolcano*. Part of this caldera contains the basin of Yellowstone Lake, which covers an area of 136 square miles (352 sq km). Underneath the basin lies a churning cauldron of melted rock, or magma, brewing 9 miles (15 km) below the Earth's surface. While another eruption is not likely to occur in next 1,000 or even 10,000 years, scientists are actively monitoring activity from the Yellowstone Volcanic Observatory (YVO). They have documented movements in the Earth, resulting in a net rise of approximately one inch (2.5 cm) per year. Recent research by the University of Wisconsin Madison concluded it was "a dying, but still potent, cycle of volcanism."

The name "Yellowstone" came from the Native American Minnetaree tribe, who called the river "*Mi tsi a da zi,*" meaning *Rock Yellow River*. French fur trappers translated this as *Roche Jaune* or "yellow stone." In 1806, John Colter, a member of the Lewis & Clark Expedition, became the first non-indigenous man to travel inside the area now known as Yellowstone. A series of expeditions followed throughout the 19th century, leading up to the Washburn Expedition in 1870. Led by General Henry Washburn, who gave his name to many of Yellowstone's famous landmarks, the expedition discovered much of the area that is now the park. In 1872, Congress passed legislation to protect the area and make it the world's first national park. President Ulysses S. Grant signed the bill that created Yellowstone National Park "for the benefit and enjoyment of the people." In 1976, Yellowstone also became an International Biosphere Reserve, and then a World Heritage site in 1978.

Yellowstone has over 10,000 geothermal features, including some 300 geysers, or two-thirds of all the geysers in the world! The other geothermal wonders are hot springs, hissing fumaroles, and bubbling mudpots. A geyser is similar to a hot spring, except that it erupts periodically, ejecting a column of hot water and steam into the air. Old Faithful is Yellowstone's most famous geyser and is located in Upper Geyser Basin. It is the most studied and most predictable geyser in the park. Erupting on average every 91 minutes, it shoots 3,700-8,400 gallons (14,000-32,000 liters) of boiling water to heights of 106-184 feet (30-55 m) for one to five minutes. Steamboat Geyser, in Norris Geyser Basin, is the tallest active geyser in the world, but is less predictable than Old Faithful. It broke a nine-year silence with a series of large eruptions of more than 300 feet (90 m) between 2000 and 2003. Geyser activity can change, and even cease, due to earthquakes, underground shifts, and other geological processes. An earthquake in 1959, measuring 7.1 on the Richter scale, actually caused Yellowstone thermal activity to increase. However, human activity, such

as oil drilling, geothermal power plants, and tossed debris, also have an impact on the park and its thermal features.

A geyser functions like a pressure cooker. It starts with surface water that seeps into the ground, filtering through fissures, cracks, and porous rock, eventually circulating to a depth of about 2 miles (3.2 km) where it meets with the magma, or molten rock. The geothermally heated water then rises back to surface, through narrow pathways that prevent cooling or vaporizing. As a result, the water becomes "superheated" and begins to boil. Steam bubbles then rise, ultimately bursting through and releasing the pressure in an eruption. Afterwards, the remaining water cools down, and the process begins all over again.

There are two types of geysers: a *fountain* geyser, like Grand Geyser, that emits a series of intense bursts, and a *cone* geyser, like Old Faithful, that sends out a steady jet. Located in the Upper Geyser Basin, Grand is the largest predictable geyser in the world, usually erupting every 6-15 hours for 12 minutes.

Beyond its thermal spectacles, Yellowstone is the finest mega-fauna habitat in the lower 48 states. Sightings may include mule deer, bighorn sheep, grizzly and black bears, moose, bison, pronghorn, coyotes, mountain lions, and beavers. The morning and early evenings are the best times to watch wildlife, and May-June offers the chance to see newborn animals. Park rangers advise staying 25 yards (23 m) away from bison and elk and at least 100 yards (91 m) away from bears; if you cause an animal to move, you are too close! A 500-pound (227 kg) grizzly bear is a danger when it is up-close and personal. The animals have also been known to block the roadways, creating bear-jams and buffalo gridlock. Keen bird watchers will find that trumpeter swans, osprey, and white pelicans make their home here, as well as a few endangered and threatened species.

A YELLOWSTONE SQUIRREL

EXTERMINATED IN 1926, WOLVES WERE SUCCESSFULLY
RE-INTRODUCED TO THE PARK IN 1995

These include Peregrine falcons, whooping cranes, and bald eagles. The bald eagles, their wingspan stretching up to 7 feet (2.1 m), can often be spotted around Yellowstone Lake. The park operates a "Bald Eagle Management Plan" to encourage breeding, and 2005 saw the largest number of eaglets born in the park so far.

Elk and bison are the two iconic symbols of Yellowstone Park. The elk are known for their mating calls, referred to as "bugling." The handsome males weigh 600-800 pounds (272- 363 kg) and grow antlers with six-or eight-point racks. The male bison (bulls) can weigh up to 1,800 pounds (816 kg) and stand six feet (1.8 m) tall at the shoulder. Both species have weathered many difficulties, some of which continue to plague the Greater Yellowstone Ecosystem.

While around 30,000 elk spend summers in Yellowstone, many venture south for the winter, to the 25,000-acre (10,117-hectare) Elk Refuge in Jackson Hole, Wyoming. Due to ranch development in the early 1900s, the elk migration patterns changed, leaving many to starve. In 1912, the government began a feeding program that now supports 8,000 elk and 1,000 bison from November to April. An unintended consequence, is that the population has ballooned beyond the size of what the landscape can naturally maintain. The overcrowding raises concerns about disease outbreaks, such as chronic wasting disease, a fatal neurological illness common in deer and elk. The solution to this dilemma is not clear, especially because the refuge now attracts 800,000 visitors a year. "We can wean the elk off feeding," says refuge manager Barry Reiswig. "Weaning the people off feeding may be more challenging."

At the same time, the bison is under threat by the Montana Department of Livestock. Half of Yellowstone's bison have been exposed to *brucellosis*, a bacterial disease that came to North America with European cattle and that may cause cattle to miscarry. Elk also carry the disease but are not considered to be a threat to livestock. The U.S. Department of Agriculture has spent $3 billion dollars over the last 70 years to eradicate this disease, and they have been successful in all but two states: Texas and Wyoming. Due to ineffective vaccines, "brucellosis-free"

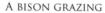

A BISON GRAZING

Around 30,000 elk spend summers in Yellowstone

Montana approved bison hunting to manage itinerant animals and to protect their livestock from the spread of disease. In 1996-1997, over a thousand bison that had traveled beyond the park's boundaries to graze were killed in Montana. As result, and in the hope of preventing further losses, the National Park Service now supervises bison movements.

One of the great success stories, though, has been the restoration of the Yellowstone wolves, also known as Northern Rocky Mountain wolves. Once thought to be harmful to the park's ecosystem, and seen as predators with no value, wolves were largely eliminated from Yellowstone by 1926. However, their eradication caused a marked increase in lame and sick wildlife, and by 1996, 31 wolves were re-introduced to the park. "The removal of a keystone species can lead to the extinction of other species," explains William Ripple, a forestry biologist at Oregon State University. The wolves have since rebalanced the ecosystem by pursuing elk, moose, and deer, thereby preventing overgrazing. Likewise, trees that suffered as a result of overgrazing, such as the cottonwood, aspen, and willow, are once again flourishing. The reintroduction of wolves, now totaling 300, has affected more than 25 species. "Part of the integrity of the ecosystem has been restored," says Christopher Wilmers, an ecologist from U.C. Berkeley. In return, ranchers are compensated for any losses caused by wolves preying on their livestock.

Letting the ecosystem run its natural course has been a tremendous learning experience for those who manage the park. In 1972, the Yellowstone Natural Fire Policy was introduced, allowing natural fires, usually triggered by lightning, to extinguish themselves. This program proved successful for 15 years, until the summer of 1988. What began as an unusually wet spring had turned into a severe drought by summer. By July 15, fires had destroyed 8,500 acres (3,439 hectares) of land. A week later, the figure was 99,000 acres (40,064 hectares). On August 20, in one single day, the fires devastated a further 150,000 acres (60,703 hectares). It was not until September that the first snows began to slow the blaze, but it took until November for the last flames to be extinguished. A total of 248 fires ravaged Yellowstone that summer, razing 793,880 acres (321,272 hectares) or 36 percent of the park. The fires killed 345 elk, 36 deer, 12 moose, 9 bison, and 6 black bears. Seven fires—the worst one caused by a cigarette—were responsible for 95 percent of the damage. Ultimately, it left a bleak, but beautiful, sight that, surprisingly, swiftly turned green once again. It appears that most of the wildlife suffered no long-term effects, quickly recovering from that red-hot summer.

It is this natural power of regeneration, inherent in our ecosystems, that amazes and inspires all who witness it. Yellowstone National Park bears testament to that, time and again.

THE 1988 FIRES RAVAGED 36 PERCENT OF THE PARK

Useful Information

General

UNESCO World Heritage Committee

7, place de Fontenoy
75352 Paris 07 SP
France
+33 (0)1 45 68 10 00 (tel)
+33 (0)1 45 67 16 90 (fax)

http://whc.unesco.org/

The United Nations Educational, Scientific and Cultural Organization (UNESCO) seeks to encourage the identification, protection and preservation of cultural and natural heritage around the world considered to be of outstanding value to humanity.

U.S. Geological Survey

12201 Sunrise Valley Drive
Reston, VA 20192, USA
703-648-4000 (tel)
888-275-8747 (toll free)

http://www.usgs.gov/

Mission: The USGS serves the nation by providing reliable scientific information to describe and understand the Earth; minimize loss of life and property from natural disasters; manage water, biological, energy, and mineral resources; and enhance and protect our quality of life.

National Park Service Headquarters

1849 C Street NW
Washington, DC 20240
(202) 208-6843 (tel)

http://www.nps.gov/

The National Park Service is a bureau within the United States Department of the Interior. Mission: The National Park Service preserves unimpaired the natural and cultural resources and values of the national park system for the enjoyment, education, and inspiration of this and future generations.

U.S. Fish & Wildlife Service

1849 C Street, NW
Washington, DC 20240

http://www.fws.gov/

Mission: Working with others, to conserve, protect and enhance fish, wildlife, and plants and their habitats for the continuing benefit of the American people.

National Parks Conservation Association (NPCA)

1300 19th Street, NW, Suite 300
Washington, DC 20036
800-628-7275 (tel)

http://www.npca.org/

Mission: To protect and enhance America's National Park System for present and future generations.

U.S. Environmental Protection Agency

Ariel Rios Building
1200 Pennsylvania Avenue, N.W.
Washington, DC 20460

http://www.epa.gov/

Mission: To protect human health and the environment in the United States.

World Wildlife Fund

1250 Twenty-Fourth Street, N.W.
P.O. Box 97180
Washington, DC 20090-7180
(202) 293-4800 (tel)

http://www.worldwildlife.org/

Mission: WWF is the largest multinational conservation organization in the world, with 5 million members worldwide and projects in 100 countries.

The Wonders

Chapter 1—Uluru / Ayers Rock

Uluru – Kata Tjuta National Park

PO Box 119
Yulara NT 0872
Australia

http://www.environment.gov.au/parks/uluru/

Cultural center:
+61 8 - 8956 1128 (tel)
+61 8 - 8956 2360 (fax)

Anangu Tours

Uluru Kata Tjuta National Park
Northern Territory
Australia
+61 8 - 8956 2123 (tel)

www.anangutours.com.au

Tours of Uluru given by the local Aborigines

Chapter 2—Easter Island

Easter Island Statue Project

http://www.sscnet.ucla.edu/ioa/eisp/

The Easter Island Statue Project is the accumulation of two decades of research and fieldwork directed by Dr. Jo Anne Van Tilburg.

PBS NOVA Program & Link:

"Secrets of Lost Empires: Easter Island"

http://www.pbs.org/wgbh/nova/lostempires/easter/

Showcases the efforts of a team of archeologists, engineers, and other experts to transport an Easter Island moai, or carved stone monolith, overland and successfully raise it onto a pedestal.

Chapter 3—The Grand Canyon

Grand Canyon National Park

P.O. Box 129
Grand Canyon, AZ 86023

http://www.nps.gov/grca/

Phone Numbers
• General Visitor Information: (928) 638-7888
• Backcountry Information Center: (928) 638-7875 between 1 pm and 5 pm Monday through Friday, except on federal holidays
• River Permits Office: (800) 959-9164 or (928) 638-7843

Grand Canyon Association

P.O. Box 399
Grand Canyon, AZ 86023
(928) 638-2481 (tel)

http://www.grandcanyon.org/

Sells publications about the Grand Canyon

Golden Gate National Parks Conservancy

Building 201, Fort Mason
San Francisco, CA 94123
(415) 561-3030, ext 2233 (tel)

http://www.parksconservancy.org/

Oversees The Habitat Restoration Team

Chapter 4—The Great Barrier Reef

Great Barrier Reef Marine Park Authority

2-68 Flinders Street PO Box 1379
Townsville QLD 4810 Townsville QLD 4810
AUSTRALIA

http://www.gbrmpa.gov.au/

+61 7 4750 0700 (tel)
+ 61 7 4772 6093 (fax)

Provides information on the latest zoning regulations

The Coral Reef Alliance (CORAL)

417 Montgomery Street, Suite 205
San Francisco, CA 94104
USA
(415) 834-0900 (tel)
(415) 834-0999 (fax)
toll free 1-888-CORAL-REEF

http://www.coralreefalliance.org/

CORAL is a member-supported, non-profit organization, dedicated to keeping coral reefs alive by integrating ecosystem management, sustainable tourism, and community partnerships.

CRC Reef Research Center

PO Box 772
Townsville 4810
Queensland, Australia
+61 7 4729 8400 (tel)
+61 7 4729 8499 (fax)

www.reef.crc.org.au

CRC Reef Research Centre is a knowledge-based partnership of coral reef ecosystem managers, researchers, and industry. Its mission is to plan, fund, and manage science for the sustainable use of the Great Barrier Reef World Heritage Area.

Australian Institute of Marine Science (AIMS)

PMB 3, Townsville MC
Townsville 4810,
Queensland, Australia
+61 7 4753 4444 (tel)
+61 7 4772 5852 (fax)

http://www.aims.gov.au/

Mission: To conduct innovative research that advances understanding of our oceans and coastal ecosystems, facilitates good stewardship of marine resources, develops sustainable wealth creation opportunities, and contributes to the discovery and development of new marine-based bio-products for industry and human health.

Chapter 5—Lake Baikal

The Trans-Siberian Railway

http://www.transib.net/

TRAVEL VISA PRO
2021 Fillmore Street (2nd floor)
San Francisco, CA 94115
Toll-free tel: (888) 470-8472, Local tel: (415) 229-3210

E-mail: info@transib.net

Source for information on the Trans-Siberian Railway and interesting, cost-effective travel solutions through Russia, and to Siberia, Mongolia, and China.

Chapter 6—The Land of the Pharaohs

PBS NOVA Program & Link:

"Secrets of Lost Empires"

http://www.pbs.org/wgbh/nova/lostempires/obelisk/

NOVA brings together a team of Egyptologists, engineers, stonemasons, and timber framers to probe the mystery of how the ancients shaped, transported, and erected their elegant obelisks.

"Mysteries of the Nile"

http://www.pbs.org/wgbh/nova/egypt/

Explore the Pyramids, temples, and other monumental architecture of ancient Egypt through riveting 360° photos shot during this NOVA/PBS Online Adventure.

Chapter 7—Machu Picchu

Andean Travel Web

http://www.andeantravelweb.com/peru/

destinations/machupicchu

Their aim to help promote Peru throughout the world by providing basic travel information about the country, highlighting some of the main tourist attractions, and putting you in touch with some of the best tour operators and hotels. The site provides information on how to make Inca Trail reservations.

Chapter 8—The Matterhorn

Tourist Office of Zermatt

3920 Zermatt
Switzerland
+41 (0)27 966 81 00 (tel)
+41 (0)27 966 81 01 (fax)

info@zermatt.ch

Matterhorn Museum

Kirchplatz, Bahnhofplatz 57
3920 Zermatt
Switzerland
+41 (0)27 967 41 00 (tel)
+41 (0)27 967 41 90 (fax)

matterhornmuseum@zermatt.ch

Chapter 9—Meteor Crater

Barringer Crater Official web site

http://barringercrater.com/

Meteor Crater Enterprises, Inc.

Interstate 40, Exit 233
Winslow, AZ 86047 USA

http://www.meteorcrater.com/

800-289-5898 (Toll Free tel)
(928) 289-5898 (Main tel)
(928) 289-2598 (fax)

Information on visiting the crater

NASA's Near Earth Object Program

http://neo.jpl.nasa.gov/

Provides information on tracking comets and asteroids

Chapter 10—Niagara Falls

The Niagara Parks Commission

Box 150
Niagara Falls, Ontario L2E 6T2
Canada

http://www.niagaraparks.com/

Maid of the Mist

(716) 284-8897 (tel)

http://www.maidofthemist.com/

Boating expeditions at Niagara Falls

Cave of the Winds Tour

(716) 278-1730 (tel)

Tour of Bridal Falls

Chapter 11—Aurora Borealis / The Northern Lights

The University of Alaska Geophysical Institute

903 Koyukuk Drive
Fairbanks, AK 99775-7320
(907) 474-7487 (tel)
(907) 474-7125 (fax)

http://www.gedds.alaska.edu/AuroraForecast/

Provides weekly auroral forecasts

Space Environment Center of the National Oceanographic Atmospheric Administration (NOAA)

325 Broadway
Boulder, CO 80305

http://www.sec.noaa.gov/

Provides estimates on position and intensity of auroral activity in real-time (includes a map of current activity in the Northern and Southern hemispheres).

The Space Weather Bureau

at NASA's Marshall Space Flight Center

http://www.spaceweather.com

Provides daily reports of geomagnetic activity and the probability of solar flares

Chapter 12—Stonehenge

The National Trust

PO Box 39
Warrington WA5 7WD
England
+44 (0)870 458 4000 (tel)
+44 (0)20 8466 6824 (fax)

www.nationaltrust.org.uk

English Heritage

PO Box 569
Swindon SN2 2YP
England
+44 (0)870 333 1181 (tel)
+44 (0)1793 414926 (fax)

http://www.english-heritage.org.uk/

Chapter 13—Yellowstone National Park

Yellowstone National Park Headquarters

PO Box 168
Yellowstone National Park, WY 82190
(307) 344-7381 (tel)
(307) 344-2005 (fax)

http://www.nps.gov/yell/

Yellowstone Volcano Observatory (YVO)

http://volcanoes.usgs.gov/yvo/

Old Faithful Visitor Center

(307) 545-2750

Yellowstone Park Foundation

222 East Main Street, Suite 301
Bozeman, MT 59715
(406) 586-6303

www.ypf.org

A nonprofit organization created by a group of concerned citizens, working with the National Park Service to preserve, protect and enhance Yellowstone National Park and to enrich each visitor's experience.

Index

Ahu Naunau   15
Ahu Tongariki   12, 17
Ahu Vai Uri   14
Alaska (state)   112, 117-118
Alps, The   84
American Falls, The (*Rainbow Falls*)
  98, 101, 104-106
Anangu   8, 11
Anasazi   25
Andes Mountains   70, 75
Arizona (state)   24
Artist Point   139, 141
Asteroids   93
Astete, Fernando   76
Aubrey, John   124
Aubrey Holes   124
Australia   6, 29-30, 33, 38, 98
Australian Institute of Marine Science
(AIMS)   33
Avebury Stone Circle   129
Avon River   130
Ayers Rock (*Uluru*)   6-11
Ayers, Sir Henry   8

Bald Eagle   145, 150
Barmasse, Hervé   84
Barringer, Daniel Moreau   93
Bas-relief   57, 62
Beaker folk   129
Bears   144, 147, 148-149, 153
Bingham, Hiram   70, 76, 81
Bison   147, 150, 153
Bluestones   124, 129
Bonaparte, Napoleon   59
Bridal Veil Falls (*Luna Falls*)   98, 106
Bright Angel Trail   28
Brucellosis   150
Brûlé, Étienne   98
Bryce Canyon   20
Buryat   43, 49

Camden, William   123
Camino Real   75
Canada   20, 98, 101, 118
Cape Burkhan   40, 43
Cave of the Winds Tour   106
Cessna Caravan   34-35
Champollion, Jean-François   53
Chephren Pyramid   59, 62
Chile   14
Chicxulub Crater   93

Circumbaikal Railway   43-44
Colorado Plateau   20
Colorado River, The   20, 25, 138-139
Continental Divide, The   141
Cook, Captain James   12, 30
Cook, Charles   139
Cook, Frederick   112
Corals   30-33
Coral Reef Alliance   30
Coronal Mass Ejections (CME's)   117
Crater (simple, complex)   94-95
CRC Reef Research Center   30
Crown-of-thorn starfish   33

De Saussure, Horace Bénédict   42-45
Druid   130, 135
Durrington Walls   129

Easter Island (*Rapa Nui, Isla de Pascua*) 12-17
Egypt   50-67, 93
Eiffel Tower   56
Elk   141, 144, 146, 147, 150, 151, 153
Endeavor, The   30
England   124
English Heritage   130, 135

Fingerprints of the Gods   51
Flinders, Matthew   29
Furggen Ridge   89

Genghis Khan   43
Geyser   141-144, 147
Giles, Ernest   8
Giza Plateau   53-56, 59
Glen Canyon Dam   25
Global warming   30-33
Goat Island   98
Grand Canyon National Park   20, 25
Grand Geyser   147
Grand Prismatic Spring   140
Grand Staircase-Escalante   20
Grant, Ulysses S.   144
Gravelet, Jean François   106
Great Barrier Reef Marine Park (GBRMP)
  33
Greater Yellowstone Ecosystem (GYE)
  141, 150
Great Lakes   38, 98
Great Pyramid, The (*Cheops*)   56, 59

Hadow, Robert   84

Hancock, Graham   51
Hanga Roa   14
Havasupai   25
Hawke, Bob   11
Heel Stone, The   124, 136-137
Hennepin, Father Louis   101
Hieroglyphics   53, 58
Hiroshima   93
HMS Pandora   30
Hoodoos   20
Hopi   25
Hörnli Ridge   89
Horseshoe Falls   98, 101, 106
Huayana Picchu   70
Hurricane Deck   106
Hydro Control Dam   106

Imhotep   56
Incan Empire   70, 75
Inca Trail, The   75, 76
Ingamells, Rex   7
International Biosphere Reserve   144
Intihuantana   76
Intipata (*Sun Gate*)   75

Johnson, Mark   25
Journal of a Trapper   141

Kaibab Trails   25
Kebira   93
Kennar, George   111

Lake Baikal   36-49
Lake Tanganyika   38
Land of the Pharaohs, The   50-67
Lintel   124, 129, 134
Lion Fish   30
Llama   76, 81
Lost City of the Incas   70
Love, Charles   14
Lyell, Charles   101

Machu Picchu   14, 68-81
Magnetic field   117
Magnetic zenith   117
Maid of Mist   106-107
Marble Canyon   21, 25
Marlborough Downs   129
Maspes, Luca   84
Mastaba   53, 56

Matterhorn, The (*Mont Cervin, Le Cervin*)
  82-89
Matterhorn Museum   89
Menkaure (pyramid)   26-34
Meteor Crater (*Barringer Crater, Canyon
Diablo Crater*)   90-95
Meteorites   93
Meteoroids   93
Mexico   20, 93
Minnetaree tribe   144
Moai   12-17
Montana (state)   141, 153
Montana Department of Livestock   150
Mont Blanc   86
Mount St. Helens   144

NASA   118
National Geographic Society   33
National Park Service, The   153
National Trust, The   135
Navajo Bridge   20, 21, 25
Nerpa Seal   38, 44
Neruda, Pablo   75
New York (state)   98, 101, 106
Niagara Escarpment   98
Niagara Falls   96-109
Niagara Parks Commission   106
Niagara River   98, 101, 106
Nile River   53, 59
Norris Geyser Basin   144
Northern Lights, The (*Aurora Borealis*)
  110-121
North Rim   20
Notes of a Tour in America   97

Obruchev, Vladimir   43
Old Faithful   144
Old Kingdom (*Egypt*)   56, 59
Olkhon Island   43-44, 48-49
Omul salmon   38, 44
Ongiara Indians   98, 106
Ontario   98, 101, 106

Paleo-Indians   25
Papyrus   53, 60-61
Patch, Sam   106
Pearson, Mike Parker   130
Peru   70
PBS NOVA   17
Phantom Ranch   25

Pharaoh (Djoser, Khafre, Khufu, Menkaure)
53, 56, 59, 62
Polynesians 14, 17
Polyps 30, 33
Powell, John Wesley 19, 25
Prisse Papyrus 53
Pulp and Paper Plant 44

Queen Victoria 84

Ranu Raraku 14, 16, 17
Rapa Nui 14, 17
Rebuffat, Gaston 83
Red Pyramid, The 56
Reinhard, Johan 69
Richards, Julian 135
Ripple, William 153
Roggeveen, Jacob 17
Rosetta Stone 53
Roman Empire 62
Royal Tomb, The 76
Rozell, Ned 118
Russell, Osborne 141

Sapa Inca Pachacuti 70
Sarsen Circle, The 126-127, 129
Scrambles Amongst the Alps 84
Selenga River 49
Shaman's Rock 43
Shark (blacktip) 32
Shoemaker, Eugene M. 91, 93
Siberia 38, 44
Skywalk 25
Solar wind 117-118
Solstice 76, 124, 130, 135
Southern Lights, The 112
(*Aurora Australis*)
South Rim 20, 24
Soviet Academy of Sciences 44
Space Environment Center, The 118
Space Weather Bureau 118
Spence, Dr. Kate 59
Sphinx, The 59, 63-64
Stakheyev, I. 38
Steamboat Geyser 144
Steinberg, Craig 33
Step Pyramid, The 56, 65
Stonehenge 122-137
Stonehenge Free Festival 130
Supervolcano 144
Swift, Dan 117

Swindon Stone, The 129, 135
Switzerland 82-87

Talus 106
Tamarisk 25
Taylor, Annie Edson 106
Temple of the Sun, The 76
Terra Australis 29
Thomas, Julian 130
Tilghman, Benjamin C. 93
Tjukurpa 8, 11
Trans-Siberian Railway 43-44
Trilithon 129, 134
Tromholt, Sophus 117
Tunguska impact 93

Ulanov, Erdeni 49
Uluru (see *Ayers Rock*) 6-11
Uluru-Kata Tjuta National Park 8
Under the Rays of Aurora Borealis 117
UNESCO 49, 76
University of Alaska Geophysical Institute
118
Upper Geyser Basin 144, 147
Urubamba River 70, 78-79, 81
U.S. Army Corps of Engineers, The 101
U.S. Department of Agriculture 150
U.S. Environmental Protection Agency, The
106
U.S. Fish & Wildlife Service 25
U.S. Geological Survey 43, 93

Van Tilburg, Jo Anne 14 17
Vivian, H. Hussey 97

Washburn Expedition 144
Washburn, Henry 144
Whymper, Edward 84, 89
Wilmers, Christopher 153
Wisconsin Glacier 98
Wolves 141, 147, 153
World Heritage 11, 49, 81, 135, 144
World Wildlife Fund 33
Wrasse 31
Wyoming (state) 141, 150

Yaki Point 24
Yarkovsky Effect, The 93
Yellowstone Caldera 144
Yellowstone Fires (summer 1988) 153
Yellowstone Lake 144, 150, 154-155

Yellowstone National Park 138-155
Yellowstone Natural Fire Policy 153
Yellowstone Volcanic Observatory (YVO)
144
Yucatàn Peninsula 93

Zermatt 82-89
Zorats Karer (*Karahunj*) 124, 135

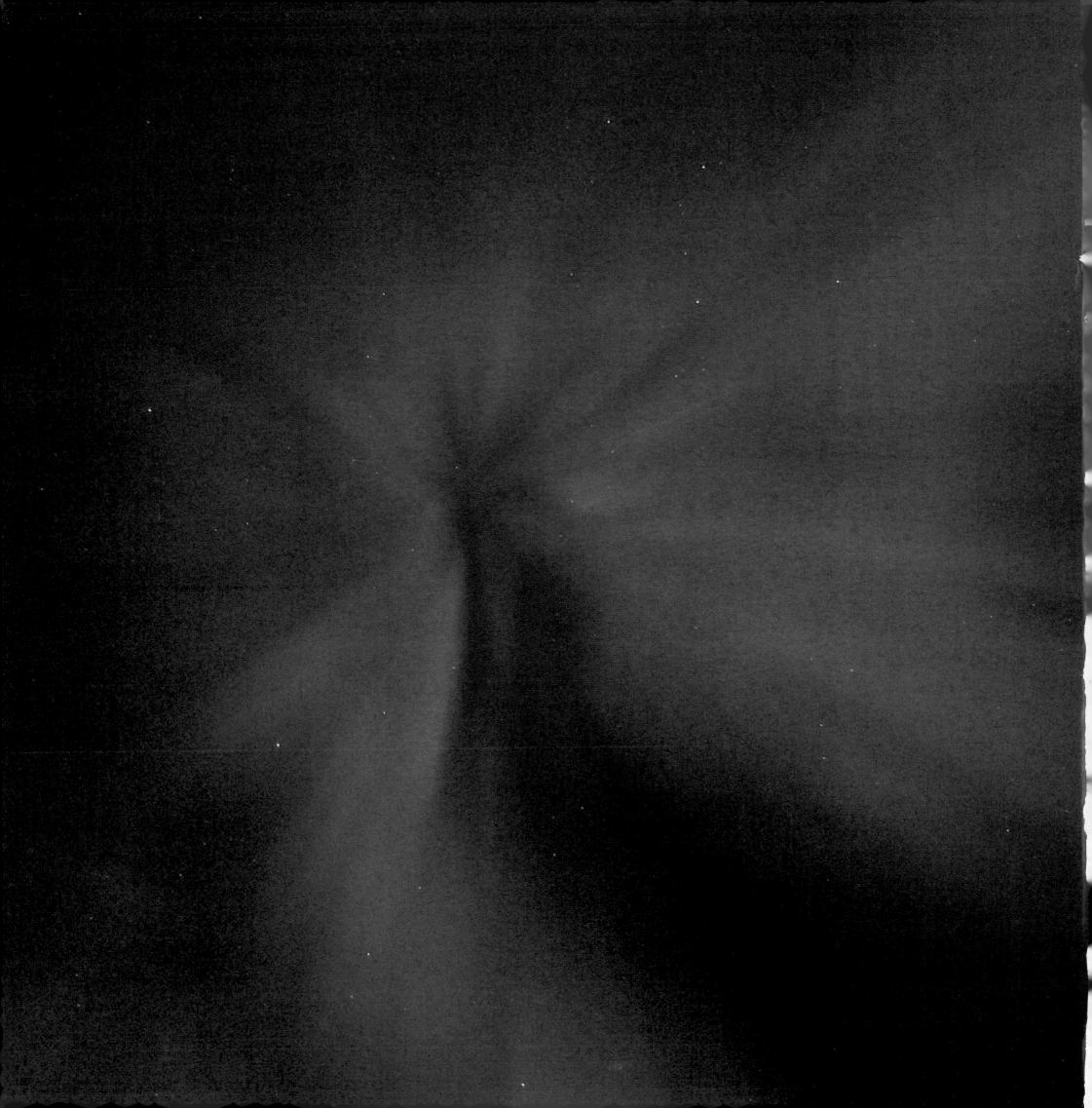